New Green Home Solutions

New Green Home Solutions

Renewable Household Energy and Sustainable Living

Dave Bonta and Stephen Snyder

ROGERS MEMORIAL LIBRARY

GIBBS SMITH

TO ENRICH AND INSPIRE HUMANKIND

Salt Lake City | Charleston | Santa Fe | Santa Barbara

First Edition
12 11 10 09 08   5 4 3 2 1

Text © 2008 Dave Bonta and Stephen Snyder
Photographs © 2008 as noted on page 144

Published by
Gibbs Smith
P.O. Box 667
Layton, Utah 84041

Orders: 1.800.835.4993
www.gibbs-smith.com

Jacket design by Black Eye Design
Interior design by Kurt Wahlner
Printed and bound in China
Gibbs Smith books are printed on either recycled, 100% post
consumer waste, or FSC certified papers.

Library of Congress Cataloging-in-Publication Data

Bonta, Dave.
  New green home solutions : renewable household energy and
sustainable living / Dave Bonta and Stephen Snyder. — 1st ed.
     p. cm.
  Includes bibliographical references.
  ISBN-13: 978-1-4236-0389-4
  ISBN-10: 1-4236-0389-3
  1. Ecological houses. 2. Dwellings--Energy conservation. 3.
Sustainable
living. I. Snyder, Stephen, 1961- II. Title.
  TH4860.B66 2008
  644—dc22
                                    2008020739

Contents

Acknowledgments

First and foremost, we want to acknowledge our agent, Jeanne Fredericks, who believed in this project from the very beginning. Her steady guidance, constant encouragement, and valuable input are a true gift to any writer. Thanks also to our publisher, Gibbs Smith, who not only shared our vision for this book but also gave us unlimited freedom in bringing it to fruition. Our editor, Hollie Keith, deserves many thanks for her infinite patience and understanding in addition to wise editorial advice. We also must thank Derek Young from the Putney Solar Store for his help with the manuscript and all of the Solar Store family for their contributions: Martin Kelly, Brian Torrico, Joe and Tony Uzabel, Pablo Fleischmann and Valerie Piedmont, Michael Ponce, Brad Vietje and Linda Ide, Peter Slota, Mark Skinder, Scott Hitchcock, Mitch Sidd, John Blittersdorf, Dee Dee Green, John Hinrichs, John Haugsrud, Scott Blood, and George Chorba. We cannot forget the USA Solar Store staff: Barbara Ryan, Diane Reynolds, and Dani Bonta, who pitched in to help this project along and patiently endured the time and energy it took away from the daily operations. Thanks also to Bruce Fiene and Mark O'Donnell, two friends who happen to be gifted photographers and who always rescue us in times of need. Thanks to SEA Solar Store owner Jack Bingham for his invaluable photography skills. Finally, a big thank-you to Ian Snyder for photography assistance, and to Melissa and Virginia Synder for endless love, patience, and support.

We have to acknowledge all of the renewable energy pioneers, writers, and experts from whom we have learned: John Schaeffer, Helen and Scott Nearing, Bill McKibben, Greg Pahl, Stephen Morris, Paul Scheckel, Dan Chiras, Nancy Taylor, Carol Venolia, Crissy Trask, James Kachadorian, Alex Wilson, Paul Gipe, and Doug Pratt, to name but a few.

We also thank the homeowners, builders, architects, designers, and renewable energy companies who made this book possible: Tom and Lisa Gaskill, Dave and Terry Coleman,

Peter and Donna Hudkins, Energie PGE, Stiebel Eltron, Al Rich and SolarRoofs.com, Cell-Tech, Sam and Christine Garst, Barbara Bourne, Andy and Stephanie Rose, Paul Wm. Moore, Jim Sargent and Vickie Anderson, Michael Frerking, David Arkin, Doug Graybeal, Ben Gordesky, Sydney and Rodney Wright, Terry Davenport, Toby Long, Tony Adrian and Marie Bossard, Gary Watrous, Mark Grantham, Rob Moody, Earl Torgerson, Mandy Metcalf, Donald Watson, Anthony Giammarino and Mona Dworkin, Emily Davis, EcoBuilders, Energy Systems and Design, Enertia Building Systems, Robert Zak and family, Bill Asdal, Bob Richer, and Stuart W. Rose.

Introduction

A Better Life

Most of the energy-based pollution we produce comes directly from our homes—when we heat, cool, and light it. Unfortunately, all of the things we love about modern life use an astounding amount of fossil fuel and send devastating amounts of pollutants into our atmosphere. Now, after years of feeling helpless, millions of ordinary Americans are asking, "What can I do?" That is the central question this book hopes to address. Obviously the problem is enormous, and clearly there is no single solution—no "silver bullet." So, what can we do individually? The good news is that because we are so personally responsible for the problem, we have tremendous power right in our own hands to change this model.

Simply stated, renewable energy design, better insulation, and more efficient appliances could reduce our household energy demand by 60 to 80 percent. By embracing conservation and renewable energy, mainstream Americans not only win their own energy independence but also make their nation more secure and help save the planet. Can you imagine a more noble enterprise? More good news is that we have vast sources of renewable energy all around us. The cheapest source of energy we have is conservation. A reduction of just 5 percent of global energy use would save the equivalent of more than ten million barrels of oil daily. Incorporating energy-efficient technology into new home construction could reduce consumption by as much as 40 percent. The indisputable fact is that if everyone began conserving today, we would see immediate results.

Americans of every stripe are becoming a part of the "green living" movement, asking what they can do as consumers of energy. This book will address the new possibilities for home power as part of a new "whole home strategy" for living green. As Henry

David Thoreau wrote: "What's the use of a fine house if you haven't got a tolerable planet to put it on?" Green living, like charity, begins at home.

Many of us in the green living movement were initially inspired by Helen and Scott Nearing, authors of *Living the Good Life*. The Nearings pioneered the back-to-the-land philosophy that blossomed during the counterculture movement of the 1960s. We believe that this book presents the next logical step in that process—living a better life—for a new, sophisticated, and technologically savvy generation.

Energy Conservation and Efficiency

Understanding Energy Usage

Before considering alternative sources for your energy needs, look for ways to reduce the demand. As in the old adage "A penny saved is a penny earned," any energy saved does not need to be generated by either fossil fuel or renewable energy. If your home is connected to the utility grid, implementing conservation and efficiency strategies means lower bills. If you are building a new home or remodeling an existing one, energy-efficient appliance and building design decisions will reduce renewable energy system expenses and lower or even eliminate your reliance on a backup power supply.

Built by Allen Associates, this residential remodel project transformed a 980-square-foot existing home on a remote two-acre parcel in the Santa Ynez Wine Country. This simple, elegant home is equipped with energy-efficient water and space heating.

First Steps

When combined with the efforts of others, your household can make a significant difference on a global scale by adopting responsible energy habits. Here are some easy steps you can take to save money and energy, reduce your CO_2 emissions, and improve indoor (and outdoor) air quality as well as your overall quality of life.

Adopt an Energy-Conscious Lifestyle—Simply being aware of what appliances are in use and of what needs to be used and when, can help you adjust habits to minimize household energy use. The most efficient practices are those that don't require any extra energy input, such as hanging clothes to dry on a clothesline. The next tier of efficiency is to install the most efficient technology and minimize use.

Determine What Your Energy Loads Are—The second step on the renewable energy journey should be to familiarize yourself with how much power your home uses and to pinpoint where your energy dollars are being spent. Study a year's worth of power bills. Try to determine how much energy is used for water and space heating, air-conditioning, and your other electrical loads. In most areas of the country, you will notice seasonal variations in energy consumption. For most American homes, heating and cooling gobbles up the greatest percentage of power—as much as one-third—and therefore deserves to be the primary focus of your efficiency planning. Water heating is usually the second-largest home energy user, followed by lighting, refrigeration, and home appliances and electronics.

The One-Degree Difference

Every degree you raise your thermostat in warm weather will lower your air-conditioning bills by around 2 percent. Lowering the thermostat by just one degree in cold weather will save you about 3 percent on heating costs. A programmable thermo-stat can trim as much as 10 percent off your space-conditioning costs. Regular maintenance and a biannual tune up will greatly improve your heating and cooling system's operation, adding more energy savings.

The architect's original plans for this remodel called for a 4,000-square-foot expansion of the existing home. The final project uses only the original footprint. This not only reduced the amount of building materials and grading required for the project but also improved long-term operation and maintenance costs for the resident, which boosts energy savings in the long run.

Use an Energy Monitor—Electric appliances can account for a sizable portion of your overall energy consumption and have a large impact on a renewable electricity system's size and cost. So-called "point-of-use" energy monitors allow you to determine how much power each appliance uses. By simply plugging the device into a socket and then plugging the appliance into the monitor, such as Watts Up? or Kill a Watt energy monitors, it will instantly show which of your appliances are energy hogs and need to be replaced with energy-efficient models.

Lots of south-facing windows and strategically placed skylights can often eliminate the need for artificial lights during daylight hours.

Watch Your Thermostat—Lowering your thermostat is the quickest way to reduce heating bills. The average homeowner can save about 2 percent of the energy used to heat a home for every degree the thermostat is lowered in winter or raised in summer. It is a common myth that it will take more energy to reheat the house than you save by keeping your thermostat set a few degrees lower. Use a programmable thermostat and set it to reduce the temperature ten degrees when you're sleeping or away from home; and when there is no possibility of freezing pipes, you can shut down your furnace completely.

Domestic hot water and space heating are provided by a compact, highly efficient Rinnai on–demand water-heating unit, which uses about half the energy of a conventional water heater.

Know Your Water Heater—Cover your water heater in an insulating wrap and lower the temperature as much as possible. Normally, a one-degree-Fahrenheit reduction in your water heater's setting will result in a 1 percent decrease in energy usage. You can opt to use a timer to turn your electric water heater off when it is not needed, but you will achieve greater efficiency by using conservation strategies such as low-flow shower-heads and insulated water heater wraps instead. If you plan to be away from home for a week or more, then it makes sense to simply shut down your system completely.

Get an Energy Audit—Professional energy auditors can help you identify the best way to spend your energy-improvement dollars. You can locate these experts through your state energy office, the Residential Energy Services Network, or the Environmental Protection Agency's Home Performance with Energy Star program (www.energy star.gov/). An energy auditor will inspect each room of your home by using devices such as an infrared camera to check for insulation voids inside a wall, and a blower door test to locate air infiltration. Always ask energy auditors what tests they will conduct, how much they charge, and if the findings will be given to you in writing. A typical home saves nearly one-third of its energy costs after conducting an energy audit and following the recommendations.

Use Power Strips—A so-called "phantom load" occurs when devices that seem to be turned off still use electricity—such as plug-in power adapters and appliances with digital clocks or indicator lights, remote controls, and instant-on capability. Although a few watts of standby energy use per appliance may sound insignificant, the total energy use of these small loads accumulates very quickly. Phantom loads in a normal American home employ more than one kilowatt hour daily—as much as a $10,000 home solar energy system provides. By using timers or power strips to control these loads, you can limit your power usage and also reduce the size of your renewable energy system. Entertainment centers and office equipment are prime examples of appliances that can easily be bundled on one power strip for convenient switching when not in use. Just remember to make your power strips easily accessible and visible so you will remember to use them.

Use power strips to shut off the "phantom loads" of unused appliances that consume one kilowatt hour daily.

Unlike just a few years ago, compact fluorescent lights (CFLs) now come in dimmable versions as well as a variety of shapes and sizes that mimic traditional lightbulbs. Switching to CFLs can lower your light bill by as much as 75 percent.

Switch to CFLs—Wherever possible, replace your old incandescent bulbs with compact fluorescent lights (CFLs). Lighting normally accounts for 10 to 15 percent of your household power bill, but switching to compact fluorescents can lower your lighting load by as much as 75 percent compared to using incandescent or halogen bulbs. An added bonus is the long life of CFLs, so you will not have to replace bulbs as often. A 10,000-hour-rated CFL burned three to four hours a day typically lasts seven years. Besides, it is estimated that 95 percent of the energy used by an incandescent lightbulb is wasted as heat with a measly 5 percent of the energy you are paying for producing light. Although its initial cost is higher, a CFL's lower energy consumption and longer life span results in significant energy and replacement cost savings in the long run. Experts recommend using CFLs everywhere except in cold areas, such as inside your refrigerator and other places where repeated on-and-off switching reduces the lifetime of the bulb and offers little in terms of energy savings.

The romantic Heim Residence in Sonoma, California, was a renovation by Carol Venolia. A covered walkway assists with blocking heat before it enters the home, therefore conserving energy that would otherwise be used to cool the home with air-conditioning.

Large windows and doorways provide cost-free illumination and passive heating through direct gain.

This totally off-the-grid home proves that energy independence does not mean sacrificing comfort or beauty.

Four Ways
To Personally Reduce Your Carbon Footprint

Drive Green—Whenever possible, join a carpool or take mass transit. When new-car shopping, carefully compare fuel economy and consider investing in a hybrid. Each gallon of gas you burn pumps about twenty-five pounds of greenhouse gases into the air. Also make sure that your tires are properly inflated. Improved gas mileage not only reduces your carbon footprint but will also save thousands of dollars in fuel over the life of your vehicle.

Buy Green Power— If you can't create all of your own renewable electricity, see if your local utility has a green power program. If not, lobby them to obtain at least half of their power from renewable resources such as wind, biomass, or solar power.

Speak Out—Public pressure works. Let your federal, state, and local politicians know you are concerned about climate change. Elected officials, especially at the local level, want to hear from concerned citizens and welcome your support when facing powerful industry lobbyists.

Remember the "3 Rs"—It may seem dull compared to the allure of high-tech renewable energy systems, but remembering to reduce, reuse, and recycle is still one of best ways to limit your carbon footprint. Products manufactured from recycled paper, glass, metal, and plastic reduce carbon emissions by reducing the energy needed to produce goods made from entirely new materials. Recycling paper and using recycled paper products saves trees, which remove carbon from the atmosphere.

Use "Daylighting"—For cost-free illumination during the day in dimly lit spaces, we recommend installing solar light tubes, a great new innovation that brings in sunlight with a series of mirrors or reflective surfaces. Skylights can work as well, but unless you are using super-efficient glass, these can let in excessive heat in the summer and draw out valued warmth in the winter. In northern climates where overheating is not as much of an issue, transparent roof panels offer a relatively affordable option for adding natural light.

Use of daylighting for indoor activities can greatly reduce the use of electric light, which accounts for 10 to 15 percent of a typical home's power bill.

Solar tubes can direct high levels of light into dark interior spaces with much less heat loss or gain of skylights.

The Kingsley-Debenham Cottage was built by Green Hammers Construction in Portland, Oregon, and designed by the homeowners. Sealing air leaks in a home with large windows and doors, such as this one, will translate to great savings for the owners.

Plug Air Leaks—The better your home is sealed, the fewer energy dollars you will spend keeping it heated in winter and cooled in summer. This seems obvious, and most of us know this instinctively, but you'd be surprised how little attention this basic energy-saving strategy gets in older homes. You will need to begin by identifying and sealing air leaks—typically found around vents, chimneys, doors, windows, foundations, and where utility conduits enter or exit the building. Tightening up your house against air leakage is perhaps the greatest cost-effective improvement you can make to reduce energy use while improving your home's comfort. Unless it is well designed, tightly sealed, and properly insulated, ductwork can account for enormous cooling and heating loss.

Use Adequate Insulation—First and foremost, make sure your attic is well insulated. Just as 40 percent or more of our body heat is lost through the head, about the same amount of home heating is lost through the attic if not properly insulated. Generally, if you have less than twelve inches of insulation, it will be wise to install more. The easiest

Although the wraparound porch shown here is a great passive cooling element, the dark roof on this home greatly increases this family's cooling expenses.

Electricity and Pollution

The nation's leading cause of industrial air pollution comes from generating electricity. As a result, our homes can often be more of a polluter than the family car. It has been estimated that around 16 percent of America's greenhouse gas emissions come from household energy consumption. According to the American Lung Association, as many as 100,000 deaths per year in the United States can be linked to air pollution.

To save energy, only run the dishwasher when it is full—and use the power- and water-miser options. Faucet aerators can also greatly reduce home water-heating costs.

time to add insulation in finished spaces is when you're making other improvements or renovations. Insulation does not function well if improperly installed, so consider hiring a professional if you have hard-to-reach spaces or are using blown-in insulation. Try not to leave gaps or compact the insulation around plumbing and electrical chases. Also make sure it contacts with all surfaces of the space where it is placed; but most of all, check that air leaks are well sealed before insulating.

Lower the Flow—In the average household, water heating is second only to space heating and cooling in the amount of energy used. By lowering water consumption, low-flow showerheads and faucet aerators can effectively lessen water heating costs. Also consider using cold water for clothes washing, and laundering only full loads. The same is true for dishwashers. Do full loads, use the water- and energy-saver settings, and open the door to air dry as much as possible. If your home is on a private

Look for the Energy Star logo when buying home appliances.

well, conserving water will also reduce the use of your electric pump, often a major energy load.

Reduce Heat Lost through Windows—Swapping your old single-pane windows with energy-efficient double- or triple-glazed ones can save substantial energy if they are fitted to stop air leaks around the frame. It should be noted that, at a small fraction of the cost, you can achieve almost as much savings by adding storm windows coupled with clear plastic insulating kits sold at hardware stores as you can with new energy-efficient windows. Again, pay close attention to air sealing when improving older windows. If you are forced to buy new windows or don't mind the expense, buy the most efficient model you can afford. Over time, they will more than pay for themselves in lower energy bills.

Household appliances—including furnaces, air conditioners, and water heaters—are responsible for approximately 90 percent of all the energy consumed in American homes.

Look for the Energy Star—Appliances bearing the Energy Star label save energy and prevent greenhouse gas emissions by meeting rigid energy-efficiency guidelines set by the U.S. Environmental Protection Agency and the U.S. Department of Energy. Energy Star products, ranging from clothes washers and freezers to air conditioners and water heaters, are measured against minimum federal efficiency standards, and the yearly savings differ depending on the appliance. Although the Energy Star label allows you to easily identify the most energy-efficient products, you should also compare energy use among similar models on the yellow Energy Guide stickers. Choose an appliance that utilizes the least amount of energy for its type.

2

Passive Heating and Cooling

A "passive" solar house supplies natural cooling and heating to condition your house without using fossil fuel or mechanical devices. The objective of all passive solar heating systems is to capture the sun's energy within the structure and to slowly release that heat throughout the day. The basic passive solar heat techniques are termed *direct gain* and *indirect gain* (which includes *thermal mass*, and *isolated gain*).

Direct Gain

Direct gain is the simplest method and is usually the least expensive. With direct gain systems, solar energy enters the home through wide areas of south-facing glass, warming floors and walls directly. Warmth from the walls and floors is radiated to the living area when the inside air temperature falls below that of the heated mass.

Clerestory windows and skylights are often employed to boost the quantity of sunlight striking the walls and floors. They do help improve the performance of the direct gain system, but as noted earlier, they have a tendency to create overheating issues in the

The Pioneer Cabin in Kirkwood, California, is a prefabricated project designed by Michael Heacock + Associates. An 800-square-foot main house with a 200-square-foot guest suite and bath make up the weekend retreat. Designed as an indoor-outdoor living space, a breezeway was created between the two structures, which opens to the sunniest spot on the site. The passive solar orientation responds to the summer sun.

Clerestory windows increase the quantity of natural light and are important passive solar elements for this home. The awnings and roof overhang outside the windows and doors help to reduce the amount of direct gain so that the interiors stay comfortable.

summer months. The amount of south-facing glass and thermal storage mass must be carefully balanced because if the windows soak up more heat than the floor or walls can take up, overheating will occur, making the living space uncomfortably warm for the occupants. Shading is then required to lower the heat gain in the warmer months. Overhangs, awnings, trellises, louvers, solar screens, and movable insulation are some ways to alleviate this problem, as most designers advocate exterior rather than interior shading to block heat before it enters the home.

Broad overhangs provide shade in the summer, along with seasonal tensile awnings. On very warm days, the owner sprays the awnings for additional evaporative cooling, since there is no air-conditioning.

In direct gain systems, the thermal storage mass can be less massive and more widely dispersed in the living area than with other passive heating methods. This permits an even distribution of heat but requires careful consideration about how the living space is utilized. Experts advise not to cover the thermal storage mass with rugs or other items that will reduce storage ability. It is also important to place furniture strategically to avoid interference with solar absorption, retention, and delivery.

Indirect Gain

Indirect gain is a term for a passive design that uses thermal mass or a sunspace to absorb solar heat and then transmit it to other areas within the structure.

Thermal Mass—Thermal mass refers to any material in the home that collects and retains heat energy. Brick, masonry, concrete, and tile absorb and then slowly release heat and generally can be integrated simply and economically into most new-home designs. Adding thermal mass allows stored solar energy to warm the home in the evening and on sunless days. In an indirect gain system, the thermal mass is located between the south-facing windows and the living space. Typical methods are an eight- to twelve-inch-thick masonry Trombe wall or a water wall of tubes or barrels placed behind the glass. During the daytime, solar energy passes through the windows and is collected in the thermal mass. The thermal mass slowly warms and then releases its heat into the living space overnight. The delay as the mass warms and then releases heat keeps the temperature of the area fairly consistent. An added benefit is that the heating of the living space occurs later in the day, when it is typically needed the most. As in all passive heating systems, a thermal mass such as a Trombe wall must be shaded during the warmer months and insulated at night during the cooler ones.

Materials with high thermal mass—which have the ability to absorb, store, and reradiate heat—work well for passive cooling. During the day, thick walls of concrete, adobe, or brick act as a heat sink, absorbing energy. At night when temperatures drop, the mass slowly releases the heat. For maximum effect, thermal mass must be exposed to

◄

Skillful deciduous landscaping on a home's south-facing side can reduce cooling costs without interfering with rooftop solar arrays.

◄

Storm shades such as the ones on this southern home can block direct sunlight from entering the windows and overheating the interior spaces.

the living spaces. High-mass buildings have up to three square feet of exposed mass for each square foot of floor area.

Isolated Gain or Sunspace—An attached sunspace or greenhouse is usually built so the collection and storage units can be shut off from the rest of the home during times of severe heat and cold. Normally, the sunspace consists of a separate room on the southern wall of the home, with an expansive glass or Plexiglas area and some type of thermal storage mass. The sunspace may extend out from the house or the house can partially surround the sunspace, allowing less heat loss and more thermal mass to be situated inside. If the sunspace provides the primary source of heat, it will need the ability to be thermally isolated from the rest of the home, with doors or windows to control excess heat from entering living spaces.

This three-walled sunspace allows daylighting as well as absorption of solar heat.

Originally a typical tract-style residence, the Fisher-Castilliano Residence in Palo Alto, California, was redesigned to take advantage of natural passive solar opportunities.

Solar Heating in Winter

While the ability to cut summer energy use presented by shading is worthwhile, efforts should be made to ensure that landscaping employed to reduce cooling costs does not negatively impinge on your prospects for effective passive solar heating. Luckily, since the sun is primarily low in the southern sky during winter, this will generally only have an effect on the south-facing area of your home's landscaping. The area that

▲
Builder Drew Maran and Lindy Small Architecture studied the site to achieve the best solar orientation, maximizing natural lighting, providing ample shading, and minimizing heat loss and solar heat gain.

▶

Large operable windows and sky-lights allow for natural ventilation and replace the need for air-conditioning within the dwelling. South-facing windows and strate-gically placed skylights can often eliminate the need for artificial lights during daylight hours.

should be unshaded is called your "solar window," or "solar access zone." For solar methods to work successfully, they should remain in full sun between nine in the morning and three in the afternoon—solar time (i.e., where the sun is during standard time, not daylight savings time). In most latitudes, this is the area from forty-five degrees east of south to forty-five degrees west of true south. During this time, the home's solar-collection areas, whether active or passive, should be free of shadows.

Winter Wind

Proper landscaping has the added advantage in winter of decreasing penetration of cold air, which can be responsible for nearly one-third of a structure's heat loss. Because higher wind speed causes greater heat loss, windbreaks that lower the wind speeds surrounding your home can greatly reduce your heating requirements. Be sure to locate your windbreak on the side of the house from which the prevailing wind blows, and do it in a way that does not interfere with your solar access zone.

Passive Cooling

Long before household air-conditioning became ubiquitous, families employed clever natural ways of keeping their homes cool in summer such as channeling breezes through strategically placed windows, building fountains in a shaded courtyard to supply evaporative cooling, and constructing their homes with stone, brick, or mud to absorb the sun's energy during the heat of the day. If heat overwhelms methods of insulation, proper building orientation, and shading, then other passive cooling methods can still be employed to effectively cool our homes.

Indeed, passive solar cooling can lessen or even do away with the need for air-conditioning in countless American homes. Simply put, passive cooling can consist of south-facing window overhangs, limiting west-facing windows, using deciduous shade trees, and employing thermal mass and cross ventilation. Surprisingly, some of the same strategies that help to warm a house in winter can cool it in summer as well.

Concrete floors collect solar heat in the daytime and slowly release the heat at night, when temperatures drop. Low-emissivity (low-e) glazing on windows keeps the heat inside the home during the winter months and outside during the summertime.

Keeping Your Cool—Many passive cooling methods eliminate heat that has built up during the day. But by stopping the sun from heating your house in the first place, you will be one step ahead. Solar energy captured by your walls, roof, and windows is the principal cause of heat gain. Lessen this with proper home orientation, reflective surfaces, awnings and various heat-blocking windows, increased insulation, and properly sized roof overhangs, as well as strategic shading with trees, shrubs, and structures for climbing plants.

Learning to Lighten Up—The more solar energy your home reflects, the cooler it will be. As you might expect, dark roofs and walls retain heat—70 to 90 percent of the sun's radiant energy, according to the Department of Energy—with the roof absorbing around one-third of this. Conversely, light-colored surfaces reflect sunlight and keep heat from being absorbed and transmitted from the attic to the rooms below.

Improving a roof's reflective quality can lower cooling costs by nearly half, depending on an attic's insulation. Experts advise installing highly reflective roofing such as white or light-colored metal roofs or tiles instead of asphalt or fiberglass shingles; even the lighter versions can still absorb significant amounts of heat. In addition to light-colored roofs, putting a radiant barrier beneath the roof or in the attic can greatly reduce heat absorption.

Using double- or triple-glazed windows with reflective films, such as low emissivity coatings (also known as low-e), help block heat energy while allowing light to pass through. In the southern states, gas-filled, double-paned windows with external tinting, low emissivity coatings, and frames using less conductive materials like vinyl and wood can greatly diminish summertime cooling requirements. Climates with hot summers and cold winters (such as in the Midwest) may need a combination of films to reflect solar energy in the summer yet still trap heat inside in the winter months.

Energy Smart Landscaping and Passive Solar

Landscaping is usually thought of in terms of improving a home's outward appearance, but when it comes to saving energy, landscaping is much more than about looks.

Removable awnings are ideal on east- and west-facing walls where only seasonal shading is desirable.

The Venice Live/Work Studio in Los Angeles, California, was designed by Davis Studio Architecture + Design. Cross breezes are created by intelligently located windows and doors and provide passive cooling throughout the structure, making air-conditioning unnecessary.

13105

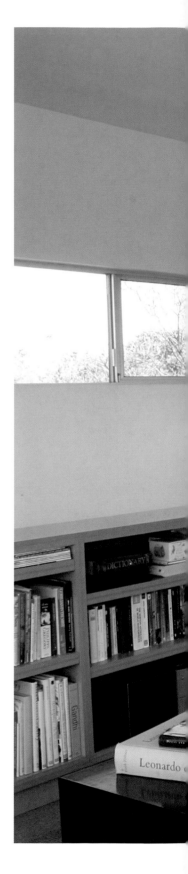

◄ ►
Windows are double glazed and aluminum framed. Double glazing increases window insulation, reducing heating and cooling requirements. Concrete slab flooring stores and radiates heat from the radiant heating system poured in the slab.

Proper landscaping can decrease a home's energy needs all year long by blocking the summer sun, funneling cooling breezes, and allowing solar warming in winter while diverting harsh winter winds.

Summer Sun

There are three key strategies landscapers use to shrink a home's cooling costs:

▶ Shading the area around the home to lower the ambient air temperature

▶ Employing thick ground covers to decrease sunlight reflected into the house and lower the surrounding ground temperatures

▶ Shading the home itself with trees, shrubs, and climbing vines

Perhaps the best thing you can do in passive cooling landscaping is planting shaded areas surrounding the house. Even though trees on the north side will not shade the house, they will reduce the temperature of air and ground around the home and lower the amount of light reflected into it. It is also important to shade the compressor of air conditioners and heat pumps as this facilitates improved performance and dampens noise from the unit. Also check occasionally to clear shrubs or leaves that may constrict airflow. Shading your roof with trees can also improve energy efficiency, but this is a landscaping strategy that should be avoided if there is a chance that roof-mounted solar hot water collectors or photovoltaic modules will be obstructed during peak solar-access times.

Natural Ventilation

Natural ventilation depends solely on the movement of air to cool the home, often through open windows alone. Since moving air promotes evaporation on the body, a home's inhabitants feel more comfortable at warmer temperatures. Windows or vents placed at opposite sides of a home help funnel breezes through the house by using cross-ventilation. Note that proper window design and use have significant effects on both direction and quantity of air movement. To promote better cross-ventilation, make a thermal chimney, or "thermosiphon," by opening windows at both the lowest and highest points in the home. Skylights and clerestory windows that can be opened can also encourage interior air currents. Last but definitely not least, ventilate your attic, a major culprit for collecting heat. Government reports show that ventilated attics are around thirty degrees Fahrenheit cooler than unventilated ones. Passive and solar-operated attic vents require no external power source and are more than sufficient for most American homes.

Open windows or skylights on the upper levels of a home create a thermosiphon—an efficient natural-cooling technique.

Evaporative Cooling

Evaporative cooling is used most effectively in hot, dry climates like America's southwestern desert. When water evaporates, the ambient air temperature decreases but relative humidity increases. As desert peoples have long known, this increased humidity makes spaces feel cooler. Fountains, pools, and transpiration from plants are all historical methods of using evaporative cooling to condition living areas. When that cooler air can be channeled into a moving current through open windows or with fans, it can also be directed to lower the temperature of interior living spaces.

Earth Sheltering

Constructing a home into the earth is another ancient method of escaping the heat of the sun. At depths below four feet, ground temperature typically stays a constant fifty to fifty-five degrees Fahrenheit year round. Earth-sheltered structures benefit from this moderate, even temperature of the earth since the ground is usually cooler than the air in summer and warmer in the winter. However, if you don't think you (or your family) would want to live underground, a comparable effect can be produced with berms, created by piling up earth against a home and installing a vapor barrier between them. In hot climates, a mere twelve to twenty-four inches of soil built on a home's west-facing side can absorb heat and greatly lessen overheating the home.

Overhangs

Properly designed roof overhangs are a common architectural element often employed on the south-facing side of the home to obstruct summer sunlight without limiting the welcome winter sun. Overhangs work best in winter on homes with a good southern exposure when the sun is at a lower angle in the sky.

A key point to bear in mind regarding roof overhangs is that they obstruct direct light. During summertime, less than half of the light hitting a vertical surface will be direct

The De La Vina Apartments in Santa Barbara, California, have wide overhanging eaves that obstruct summer sunlight without limiting the welcome winter sun.

sunlight. The rest is reflected and diffused light not obstructed by the overhang, so plan to implement other cooling methods discussed in this section for maximum benefit.

Interior Shade

Although interior shade techniques are not as efficient at blocking the sun's energy before it warms the home, it can nevertheless be a valuable addition to exterior shading. Since curtains and blinds are used on most windows anyway, choose heavy, insulated window treatments that do double duty to block out unwanted heat in summer and keep in warm air during winter.

Reflective Surfaces

Reflective films and coatings that attach directly to the windowpane can filter out more than 80 percent of the sun's rays. Available coatings include those that can be attached as needed or that permanently adhere to the glass. It should be noted, however, that because permanently attached coatings will block solar heat from entering year round, they should not be installed on south-facing windows if you intend to use them to collect passive solar energy.

Radiant Barriers

Radiant barriers are a novel way to obstruct solar heat from warming the home in summer, especially where there is a lack of shade. Radiant barriers are simply a layer of reflective metal placed in an airspace between the roof and the attic insulation. It reduces the heat energy entering the building by reflecting radiant energy from the sun.

Reducing Heat Generation

As with all green living strategies, conservation should come first. The same is true for keeping your home cool. By reducing the amount of heat the occupants of a house create in warm weather, the less effort will be needed in trying to reduce it.

A considerable amount of the unpleasant heating of our homes in the summer springs from cooking meals or doing laundry. Although we cannot be expected to avoid the use

Five Components of A Passive Solar Home

According to the U.S. Department of Energy, the following five fundamentals are needed for a full passive solar home design. Each performs a separate function, but all five must work together for the design to be successful. For more information, see the DOE's Energy Efficiency and Renewable Energy Web site: http://www.eere.energy.gov.

Aperture (Collector)—This is a large area of glazing through which sunlight enters the house. Normally, the aperture should face within thirty degrees of true south and should not be shaded from 9 a.m. to 3 p.m. during the home heating season.

Absorber—An absorber is an exposed heat-collecting component (masonry wall, tile floor, water container, or partition) that sits in direct sunlight.

Thermal mass—This is a component that retains the heat from sunlight. The distinction between an absorber and a thermal mass is that unlike an absorber, which is exposed to direct sunlight, the thermal mass is the material below or behind that surface that stores the solar energy.

Distribution—This is the manner whereby stored solar heat is distributed from the collection and storage components to the various living spaces in the home. A purely passive solar design only uses the three natural heat transfer methods—conduction, convection, and radiation. However, some homes employ fans, ducts, and blowers to distribute the heat through the house.

Controls—Roof overhangs, operable vents and dampers, low-emissivity (low-e) blinds, awnings, and thermostatically controlled fans can be used to shade an aperture and manage heat flow during summer months.

of modern conveniences completely in summer, wise use of them can go a long way in keeping a home cooler. Wash only full laundry loads and use cold water whenever possible. It is the agitation, not the hot water and soap, that does most of the cleaning anyway. You will save tons of energy required to heat the water, reducing the addition of hot, humid air into your living space. Use a clothesline if possible, or at the very least, do laundry in the early morning or at night, when it is cooler.

This custom 3,800-square-foot home stands on five acres in Colorado with magnificent views of the Front Range of the Colorado Rockies. Davis Studio Architecture + Design carefully oriented the house so that it takes advantage of the sun's passage across the sky. Natural ventilation is used to remove hot air from the interior through the use of a solar chimney. As warm air rises through the house, an updraft is created that draws cool air in and ventilates heat at the top of the central tower, through multiple operable windows.

3

Solar Electricity

The quantity of energy from the sun that reaches the earth is astounding. All the energy of the earth's known oil, coal, and natural gas reserves is equaled by the energy from just three weeks of solar energy. Indeed, it has been estimated that the solar energy reaching the earth in a typical day can provide all the power needs of the earth for a full year. The good news is this solar power is now more affordable and more widely available to homeowners than ever before.

Photovoltaic (PV) energy harnesses the power of sunshine to supply the home with electricity. PV power is reliable and virtually maintenance free, does not produce greenhouse gases, and, above all, is renewable as long as the sun keeps shining.

The three basic types of silicon solar cells are single crystal, polycrystalline, and amorphous.

PV power is reliable and virtually maintenance free, does not produce greenhouse gases, and, above all, is renewable as long as the sun keeps shining. A one-kilowatt PV system prevents 150 pounds of coal from being mined and more than a hundred gallons of water from being consumed each month.

- Single-crystal cells are produced in long cylinders and sliced into round or hexagonal wafers. This process is energy intensive and wasteful, but it produces very efficient cells—as much as 25 percent under ideal conditions.

- Polycrystalline cells are manufactured of molten silicon formed into ingots or thin sheets, which are then sliced into squares. Production costs are less than for single-crystal cells, but the efficiency of the cells is poorer—approximately 15 percent. An advantage with this type is that since the cells are square, they can be fitted together more closely.

- Amorphous silicon (a-Si) is a method in which silicon is sprayed in a thin film onto a metal or glass backing, greatly simplifying the manufacturing process. This produces the least expensive solar option, but the trade-off is very low efficiencies of around 5 percent.

Solar Module Efficiencies

The sun typically delivers 1,000 watts per square meter measured at noon on a clear day and at sea level. This is defined as a "full sun" and is the benchmark by which modules are rated and compared. In reality though, altitude, dust, pollution, seasonal variations in the sun's angle, humidity, and ambient temperature all influence how much solar energy a photovoltaic (PV) module really collects. The common assumption in the industry is that most home sites will only average about 85 percent of full sun, except for sites over 7,000 feet above sea level, where efficiencies greater than one kilowatt per square meter can be achieved.

PV Life Spans and Maintenance

Simply put, solar modules last a very long time. The oldest residential modules are still functioning perfectly after thirty years, as are most of the modules on earth-orbiting satellites that have been in the harsh environment of space for decades. Nearly all solar modules now feature fifteen- to twenty-five-year warranties, reflecting the widespread industry confidence in their longevity.

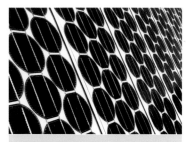

Gathering solar energy through PV panels isn't enough; we need to be sure not to waste that energy in other ways. For instance, a hot water drip from a leaky faucet at the rate of one drop per second could waste 2,300 gallons of hot water per year, as much as a forty-watt bulb left on twenty-four hours a day, seven days a week.

Besides photovoltaic cells for capturing the sun's energy, this home has large expanses of glass that save energy by inviting the sun to both warm and light the home.

Refrigeration in a solar-powered home is usually the largest user of electricity. The energy-efficient Sun Frost refrigerator can run on photovoltaic and battery power.

Having no moving parts makes PV modules virtually maintenance free. An occasional rinse with a garden hose when they are cool to the touch is usually the only cleaning they will ever need.

Powering Appliances

Any appliance that you can run with utility-supplied power theoretically can be powered by solar. However, 240-volt AC appliances that draw huge energy loads such as furnaces, air conditioners, electric water heaters, and stoves are considered impractical to run with PV power since the system costs to create that much electricity generally outweigh the money saved. However, other large-load items that cycle on and off quickly, such as deep-well pumps, can be run on solar power with no problem. PV users, particularly those living off the grid with no utility backup, often opt to use alternatives such as propane or natural gas for hot water, space heating, and cooking as well as the passive solar strategies discussed earlier. Electric heat, refrigerators, and lights are normally the main 120-volt AC energy users in a home, and these items, as noted in the conservation and efficiency chapter, should be upgraded with the most energy-efficient models possible.

The accepted belief is that for every dollar spent replacing inefficient appliances, you save three to four times that in renewable energy system costs needed to power them. So you can see that energy conservation is crucial and can really pay off when considering a renewable energy system.

PV for Water Heating and Space Heating

Because photovoltaics convert solar energy into electricity at such a low efficiency of around 15 percent, heating water and living spaces is not a very practical use of solar electric systems. Passive solar—the direct heating of air or water by the sun—is much more efficient for heating applications than photovoltaics. A better alternative is to use a solar hot water or hot air system as discussed in the Solar Hot Water Heating and Solar Space Heating chapters.

Polycrystalline solar cells are formed in large blocks made up of many crystals. They are significantly cheaper to manufacture than monocrystalline (single-crystal) solar panels but are also slightly less efficient.

This home in Los Angeles, California, was designed by owner Russell Johnson to last for over 150 years, at which point the building can be disassembled and recycled.

Photovoltaic (PV) roof panels collect heat
from the sun and supply the home with
electricity. The walls, which are made of
Rastra insulating concrete units, also
absorb solar energy and act as a heat sink.

Orienting Solar Modules

To properly install a PV system, it is essential to be aware of the siting and tilt requirements. PV modules must be aligned and angled to attain the greatest solar radiation and to avoid shading. Evaluating these factors is crucial in establishing if your planned site is appropriate for collecting solar power and in guaranteeing that the system functions efficiently.

A PV module collects the most solar energy when it is at a ninety-degree angle to the sun. If at all possible, it should be angled to track the sun's elevation during the course of the year and rotated to follow the sun's apparent path across the sky during the day. East-west tracking is achievable for a PV system with active or passive tracking systems, which can deliver upwards of 30 percent more power, depending on the season.

For fixed PV systems without tracking, solar modules are installed facing true south (the location of the sun at noon during standard time), where they can receive the greatest level of solar radiation throughout the day. There are exceptions to true south siting where conditions dictate, such as coastal areas where morning fog requires a slight shift to the west to optimize afternoon solar collection.

Solar modules can be easily and attractively mounted to almost any roof style.

Magnetic Declination

Due to the variation of the earth's magnetic field from true south, a compass reading of south can vary as much as twenty-two degrees from true south, depending on the location. This variance, or magnetic declination, is usually represented as the degrees magnetic north differs from true north. Therefore, solar modules must be installed with an adjustment made to account for this declination to achieve the best solar access.

Shading and the "Solar Window"

After true south is accurately determined, the site should be checked by your installer to establish if trees or structures to the south will limit solar access at any time during the year. Although solar modules do not need access to the sun from dawn to dusk, they must be unobstructed from 9 a.m. to 3 p.m. when more than 80 percent of the

Even minor shading on solar modules, as seen here, can drastically reduce or eliminate power output.

sun's energy hits the earth. Because they are wired together in a string like Christmas tree lights, in most PV systems, shading of just one cell will drastically reduce the power production of the entire module by 75 percent or more. Even the shade caused by the bare limbs of a tree in winter can cause enough shading on a PV collector to eliminate its effectiveness. Solar hot water and solar hot air collectors are not as sensitive to shading, but as a general rule, all solar energy systems should be installed to maximize solar access for as many hours as possible.

Types of PV Systems

Grid-connected solar systems provide quiet and trouble-free electricity. Systems with battery backup provide power during outages, and all of these systems can help you contribute to the fight against global climate change and increase your independence from expensive, vulnerable, and polluting sources of energy. Which system you choose will depend on a number of factors including your lifestyle, power needs, location, and budget.

Basic Grid-Tie Systems—with and without Batteries—For most grid-tie systems, we usually recommend against using batteries. Inverters designed for grid-tie as well as batteries are often less efficient than those purposed for one system type or the other. In addition, charging and discharging batteries wastes 15 percent or more of the energy generated by a PV system. Battery systems are also considerably more expensive, adding around one-quarter to one-third to the price of your system. In addition, batteries have to be replaced every seven to ten years, depending on their level of use and care, and they must be regularly maintained. Nevertheless, the current and future reliability of your local electric utility as well as your own personal needs should be taken into account when designing your system. Batteries offer a substantial benefit if

Architect Dale Pekerek of The Fine Line and Campanelli Construction worked together to bring several solar features to these apartments in Santa Barbara, California: each unit is equipped with solar electric stub outlets, on-demand water heaters, and Energy Star appliances.

power outages are frequent in your area or if you work from home or rely on medical equipment that needs electricity.

Grid-Tied Solar Electric Systems—Grid-tied solar electric systems, also known as grid-tied PV, grid-intertied, or utility-intertied PV systems, generate electricity and send it into the electric utility grid, offsetting your home's power consumption and, in some cases, literally spinning the electric meter backwards. Life on a grid-tied system

Tile on the kitchen floor is an indirect gain feature that allows the absorption of solar heat through windows above the sink and a clerestory window. Natural "daylighting" eliminates the need for electric lighting, which accounts for 10 to 15 percent of a home's power bill.

The 5th Street Pads in Berkeley, California, are contemporary green town homes that use rational site organization, smart technologies, and environmentally friendly materials. Photovoltaic panels are metered directly to each unit.

is the same as living solely on grid power, except that a portion or all of the energy you consume comes from the sun. In several states, the utility offers a credit to the homeowner for the electricity generated but not used. This credit is then applied in months when the homeowner creates less than is used. This agreement is termed "net metering" or "net billing" and is one of the best reasons to go solar.

Off-Grid PV Systems—Solar electric systems not connected to a utility are termed "off-grid" or "stand-alone systems." The two main types of stand-alone systems are direct systems, which use the PV electricity as it is generated, and battery backup systems, which can store solar-generated energy for later use. Although some off-grid homeowners opt to use direct current (DC) appliances, most off-grid systems with a battery backup have an inverter to convert the DC electricity from the solar panels to alternating current (AC) so the more widely available AC appliances can be used.

System Components

PV systems are composed of several interconnected components to collect, transmit, convert, store, and manage the power created. One of the major strong points of PV systems is their modularity. When your power requirements change, components can be upgraded or added to boost capacity. Below is a brief overview of the components in a typical solar electric system.

Solar Modules—Typically, these are made up of a sheet of glass enclosing the solar cells that convert sunlight into electrical power, and a waterproof backing mounted in a metal frame. A few modules are now manufactured with a non-glass glazing over an aluminum back without the frame.

Solar Array—A solar array is one or more PV modules connected in a series. Arrays are mounted on metal roof mounts or a pole in the yard and angled to face the sun.

Battery Bank—This consists of several deep-cycle batteries connected together. These batteries store the electricity generated by the solar array, which is released as needed.

Charge Controller—Charge controllers primarily keep your batteries at a proper charge level and prevent them from overcharging.

Inverter—The inverter converts DC power generated by the solar array into AC power. An inverter is necessary if you want to run AC appliances.

Safety Fusing and Disconnects—Safety and disconnect components supply the interconnections and standard safety features required for electric power systems. These consist of appropriately sized wiring, fuses, combiner boxes, various switches, circuit breakers, system monitors, and power meters.

Battery Sizing

Off-grid PV systems require high-quality, deep-cycle batteries designed for a steady release of power, like those used in golf carts and boats. Automobile batteries, on the other hand, are designed to provide cold-cranking amps and a sudden burst of power and not to be discharged deeply, so they will wear out quickly in a typical off-grid solar situation. Because these deep-cycle batteries are expensive, extending their life is essential. This is accomplished by discharging the battery just a little before it is recharged. A well-designed battery system will be sized so that the batteries are regularly discharged only about 20 percent. In long sunless periods, care should be taken not to discharge the battery bank more than around 80 percent. You can always add more batteries as needed, but, again, this will add considerably to your system cost. Off-grid systems with battery banks need a good-quality charge controller to ensure that the battery is never overcharged. To keep your batteries from being drained, a load controller can be added to your system, and some charge controllers

▼ ▶

Solar power is estimated to provide up to 85 percent of all electrical energy for these apartments. Compared to fossil fuel–generated electricity, each kilowatt of solar power offsets between three to five thousand pounds of carbon dioxide each year.

have built-in load controllers. Overcharging as well as excessive discharging can cause severe and lasting battery damage.

Mounting Racks

Mounting racks provide a raised area to secure your PV arrays, keeping them set in place and properly oriented. Racks also allow airflow around the panels to keep them cool, which increases efficiency. Panels may be mounted on the roof, on a steel pole anchored in concrete, or on a frame on the ground. Generally, PV arrays in areas with limited yard space or excess shade obstructions are installed on a south-facing roof. This is often the most attractive and best space-saving option, but it may be controlled by neighborhood ordinances or local homeowner associations. In rural areas with lots of room, pole- and ground-mounted arrays are a frequent choice, especially if this increases solar access or if solar panels on the roof are out of character with an older home. PV mounting racks may include additional features, such as adjustability. Adjustable mounting racks allow one to change the angle of PV modules throughout the year to keep them more in alignment with the sun. However, adjusting the angle only improves a system's productivity by a few percentages, and on roof-mounted arrays, most homeowners rarely consider it worth the extra effort and danger of working on the roof.

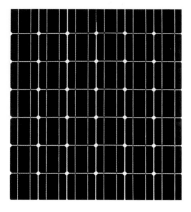
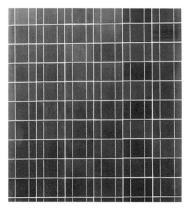

Kilowatt Meters

The vast majority of grid-tied homes will have power flowing from the grid as well as back to the electric utility. A bi-directional kilowatt-hour meter can simultaneously track how much electricity flows each way so you will be able to monitor how much electricity you are consuming and how much you are generating. Your utility will probably supply you with this meter at little or no cost.

Back-Up Generators

Off-grid solar systems can be designed with enough battery storage to supply power during extended cloudy periods. However, sizing a system to cover several cloudy weeks during the winter will give you an oversized, very costly system that will hardly

Available solar modules vary widely in style and wattage and require only two to four years to match the energy that went into manufacturing them.

ever be used to full capacity. To avoid unnecessary expense, we advise our clients to size their systems for moderate use but consider a back-up generator, preferably one that uses biodiesel to survive long cloudy periods. Unfortunately, gas and diesel generators are loud and smelly unless they can be kept in a well-insulated area away from the main living spaces. However, a properly sized PV system should need only a few days of back-up generator use per year.

Tracking Devices

PV modules are sometimes mounted on tracking mechanisms to collect slightly more solar energy. A single-axis tracker simply tracks the east-to-west progress of the sun as it moves across the sky. In addition to east-west tracking, a double-axis tracker angles the module to follow the sun's changing altitude.

There are two main types of trackers: passive thermally operated models and active electrically operated ones. The chief benefit of passive trackers is the lack of electrical parts to malfunction. Another benefit of thermal trackers is that they are usually less costly than active trackers. Passive trackers have several disadvantages, however. For example, because the heat of the sun powers them, they respond slowly, especially in cold weather. Another issue is that passive trackers don't follow the seasonal altitude changes of the sun and have to be manually aligned for summer and winter declination. Active trackers, on the other hand, use photoelectric sensors to establish the angle of the sun. One of the other main benefits of this type is that they are more accurate in tracking the sun. A second advantage of electrically operated trackers is that they are powered by electricity, not the sun's heat. This makes this type of tracker more accurate in climates with cold winters.

In summary, trackers can boost your system's power output by as much as 40 percent, but using a tracker is only cost effective if the value of the extra energy gained with the tracking system exceeds the cost of buying, installing, operating, and maintaining your tracker. Your solar installer or dealer will be a great asset in helping you decide if tracking is appropriate for you.

Space Considerations

The area needed by a solar electric system is determined by the power yield of the system and the kind of system you have installed. Most home systems need as little as fifty square feet for what we call a "camp" system, or 1,000 square feet or more for premium systems. A typical two-kilowatt system used by the average family of four would take up around 150 to 200 square feet. If your site restricts the size of your PV system, you may need to install more efficient PV modules. Higher efficiency translates to less surface area for the same amount of solar power, but bear in mind that higher efficiency means higher cost.

Building Integrated PV

An exciting new innovation called Building Integrated Photovoltaic (BIPV) uses the entire roof surface of a home as a solar collector and can appear indistinguishable from a standard shingle, slate, or standing-seam roof. One idea that is growing more popular is BIPV where the PV can be built into a building's walls as well as the roof, displacing building materials. Several BIPV products already exist, incorporated into metal roofing, roof tiles, curtain wall systems, and atrium glass.

Many of the most exciting new solar products are using thin film PV. Thin film PV cells are manufactured using processes that allow incredibly thin layers of semiconductor PV materials to be made as flexible modules that conform to curved surfaces or to be used where rigid PV cells cannot. The amount of semiconductor material used to produce thin film PV is much less than that used to produce crystalline PV, so it can be produced faster and cheaper. At present, thin film PV modules are much less efficient than crystalline PV, but that situation undoubtedly will change in the not-too-distant future.

Scalability

One of the most attractive features of solar power is its scalability—the ability to add components easily as your budget allows or as your needs change. You may consider starting out with a micro system to supply only a fraction of your electrical loads. The rest of your power is purchased from your utility until you are ready to expand your system by adding more modules.

▲
Building-integrated photovoltaics, or BIPV, work surprisingly well on this colonial-style home, mimicking the look of slate.

▶
Although solar modules do not require exposure to the sun all day long, they should be free from shading from 9 a.m. to 3 p.m., when more than 80 percent of the sun's energy hits the earth.

Location

Where you live directly affects the price of your system. Areas outside the sunbelt require bigger systems to produce the level of power a smaller system in a sunny climate can generate. Many areas of the Southwest receive an annual average of more than six peak sun hours daily, while the Pacific Northwest receives less than four. To find the peak sun hours in your area of the country, check the Renewable Resource Data Center's Web site in the Resources section at the end of this book. Weather and other factors unique to your site will influence your PV system size and production capacity since PV modules function better in cooler weather and less effectively when it is hot.

Proper System Sizing and Cost

A typical single-family home consumes an average of thirty-four kilowatt hours per day. That adds up to 12,000 kilowatt hours a year. At twelve cents per kilowatt, the average American pays $1,440 to the local utility. A PV system in most of the country will collect energy at an annual average of approximately 4.5 hours per day. Given these realities, unless you first cut your power consumption to shrink this load, you would need at least a six-kilowatt array. At a reasonable estimate of $10 per watt installed, a PV system of this size would cost you $60,000 before incentives, tax credits, and rebates. Obviously, a more sensible move would be to install a smaller less-expensive system in the two- to three-kilowatt range after doing all you can to practice the conservation and efficiency methods discussed earlier. Then have your PV system matched to your critical power loads, such as lights, space heating, and water pumping, and try to avoid using noncritical appliances during power outages unless you have backup power.

Areas outside the the sunbelt, such as the Pacific Northwest, will require larger systems to produce the amount of energy a smaller system in a sunny area, such as the Southwest, can make. Your local renewable energy retailer should be able to help answer questions about system sizes needed in your area.

Increase Your Home's Value with Renewable Energy

A renewable energy system can slash or eliminate the energy operating cost of your home and offer a hedge against electric rate inflation. Several home-appraisal organizations have suggested that, on average, every dollar saved on your monthly electric bill by an energy-saving renovation such as a solar system adds $20 in resale value to the home. Studies in California seem to bear this out, showing that homes with renewable energy systems command higher prices, usually more than the added cost of the system.

It has been estimated that every watt-hour eliminated from your daily use in a PV system will reduce your cost by $3 to $4. With close attention to energy efficiency and conservation, most home-sized PV systems cost between $15,000 and $25,000, depending on the size of the family and its lifestyle. Renewable energy rebates and tax incentives will shrink your cost considerably—often by as much as half. Your final cost depends on a number of things, such as whether your house is an older structure or is newly built, and whether your modules will be building integrated, pole mounted, or roof mounted. Cost may also vary according to the brand of products you buy, your renewable energy retailer, the area of the country where you live, and the installer you choose.

In the final analysis, solar electric power is not cheap. Although PV power now costs a fraction of what it did thirty years ago, the cost measured over its life span is still more than twenty cents per kilowatt hour. Renewable rebate programs from your state and your power company make PV cheaper, but this is still about double the average cost of grid-supplied electricity in most areas of the country—although this is changing quickly. Renewable energy of all types requires a high initial investment, but you are buying years of electric bills in advance. Your monthly power bills will shrink or even disappear, but be aware that the initial cost of installing solar power could be considerable.

4

Solar Hot Water Heating

Solar hot water systems are dependable, reasonably priced, and attractive. Clean trouble-free solar domestic hot water (SDHW) will let you shrink your energy consumption and give you freedom from fossil fuel–based heating sources. A solar hot water system can supply nearly all of your hot water needs, even in cold regions of the country.

The average American home spends anywhere from 20 to 40 percent of its energy dollars on water heating. Although PV systems get the most attention in the media, in most households, a solar hot water system will yield more energy at a considerably lower price. Believe it or not, solar hot water collectors have more than triple the efficiency of PV modules in producing energy.

Collector racks can be mounted at steep or shallow angles, depending on the orientation of the sun and the seasonal demand for energy.

How SDHW Works

Solar water heating systems basically consist of solar collectors and a storage tank. There are two general categories of solar water heating systems: active systems, which have pumps to circulate the hot water, and passive systems, which rely on thermosiphoning

▲ ▶

This traditional suburban home in Palo Alto, California, was renovated by builder Drew Maran and Heidi Hansen Architecture. A solar domestic hot water system greatly reduces this family's energy consumption.

to move the liquid. In thermosiphon systems, water flows through the system when hot water rises and cold water sinks. The collector has to be installed below its storage tank so that hot water will rise to the tank. These systems are reliable and long lasting, but your roof must be able to support the substantial weight of the storage unit. On average, passive solar water heating is less expensive, longer lasting, and more reliable than active systems but is generally considered less efficient.

Both kinds of solar water heaters need super-insulated storage tanks. In a single-tank system, a conventional backup heater is combined with the solar storage into one tank. In a double-tank system, preheated water is held in storage before it flows to a conventional water heater.

There are three basic styles of solar hot water collectors:

Integral Collector Storage—Also referred to as an ICS or "batch" system, these hold black tanks or tubes in an insulated box with a glass top facing the sun. Cold water flows through the collector, which heats it. The heated water then flows to a conventional water heater, so there is also a reliable backup source of hot water. ICS systems can be used only in mild frost-free areas of the country, where the exposed pipes of the system won't freeze in winter. This type of system is not as widely available as the following two but can be homemade quite easily.

Flat-Plate Collector—These are insulated weatherproof boxes that enclose a black absorber plate with a plastic or glass cover. This is the most widespread type of collector and is often considered the most efficient in nearly all climates.

Flat-plate collectors, as shown in this thermosiphoning domestic solar hot water system are, generally more efficient than evacuated tubes in all but the most severe northern climates.

75

Evacuated-Tube Solar Collectors—These have parallel rows of clear glass tubes. Each tube contains a vacuum-sealed outer tube and an absorber tube inside attached to a metal fin. The fin absorbs solar energy but doesn't allow the heat to radiate back out. These collectors were originally used mostly in commercial buildings but are rapidly gaining popularity, especially in colder regions where, theoretically, they can provide greater efficiency in winter months.

Sizing Solar Hot Water Systems

As with PV power, the level of hot water that solar energy will produce depends on the size and type of the system, the climate, and the quality of your solar window. Solar domestic water heating almost always needs a backup system for cloudy days and periods of higher usage. Conventional water

Located in a lush orange grove in Santa Paula, California, the Burns Residence is a newly built single-family home designed and built by Thompson/Naylor Architects and Allen Associates. There is a solar water-heating system with natural gas and an on-demand heating system for backup.

heaters provide reliable backup and often are part of the solar hot water system anyway. Many homeowners opt to install a super-efficient tankless, on-demand water heater as a backup.

Before installing a solar hot water system, research what your possible savings might be. Energy auditors and renewable energy retailers can test your house to establish how to reduce your energy consumption and if a SDHW system is appropriate for your home. If you then decide to purchase a system, explore a number of alternatives before selecting the type that best suits your home. A high-quality, well-maintained SDHW system should last for more than twenty years, so plan for the long term.

High-quality and properly installed SDHW systems are energy efficient, long-lived, and dependable. Designs can range from straightforward systems relying on gravity and thermosiphoning to more complex systems requiring heat exchangers, controllers, and pumps. Although they require a higher initial investment than conventional water heaters, they will dramatically reduce fuel consumption and can have a speedy payback of five to ten years.

If your energy use is limited or can be trimmed, your hot water needs may be supplied with a relatively small system. Small hot water units are less expensive and offer a faster payback through energy savings, but it should be noted that the installation costs of a small system are similar to a moderately sized one. Obviously, your system's size depends on your family's hot water consumption; generally, you will need ten to twenty square feet of collector area per household occupant. You will also need approximately two gallons of storage capacity for every square foot of collector area. For a typical family of four, this translates to two or three flat-plate collectors or sixteen evacuated tubes and at least 100 gallons of storage tank capacity. In most locations, this averages out to around $6,000 to $7,000 in total installed costs before deducting rebates and incentives.

Several inches of urethane foam in SDHW storage tanks, such as this Stiebel Eltron model, ensure that hot water stays hot and standby heat loss is minimized. These typically come either with a single heat exchanger that can be used for solar applications with some form of external backup heater, or with dual heat exchangers for connecting to both a space heating boiler and solar thermal collectors.

Solar Hot Water Installation

As with other solar energy systems, orientation of collectors is essential, and solar hot water collectors function best when facing true south. While angling the collectors to match your local latitude will increase productivity, mounting collectors flat against a south-facing roof will only minimally diminish its efficiency. As with PV, it is just as important to mount the collectors where they will not be shaded from 9 a.m. to 3 p.m.—the peak solar window.

Proper installation of domestic solar water collectors depends on several issues and is not generally recommended as a do-it-yourself project. Key issues to consider include solar access, regional climate, and local building codes, as well as health and safety issues. In addition, many states require a licensed installer do the work in order to collect rebates and incentives.

Another advantage SDHW has over other renewable energy systems is its low profile. Because so few panels or tubes are needed by the average family, they blend in better with home exteriors.

A high-quality, well-maintained SDHW system should last for more than twenty years.

◄

Shown is an evacuated tube solar domestic hot water collector.

▶

Solar domestic hot water typically requires fewer collectors than solar electric systems—an advantage where aesthetics demand a cleaner roof profile.

Everything Solar Is New Again

Far from being a new technology, solar hot water collectors have been around for more than a hundred years and were wildly popular in Florida and Southern California during the 1920s and 1930s before cheap oil and gas displaced them. Today, Israel is the world leader in solar water heating thanks to a law passed in the Knesset after the 1973 oil embargo mandating their use in all new homes. Today, more than 90 percent of Israeli homes employ solar water heaters.

5

Solar Space Heating

Whether you plan to heat a single room or an entire house, solar space heating can trim your costs easily and efficiently. By heating your house with sunshine, solar space heating systems lower your consumption of traditional heating fuels by supplementing or even replacing your current home-heating method.

Solar Space-Heating Options

The typical American home uses more than 60 percent of its entire yearly energy budget for space and water heating at a cost of nearly $1,000. Luckily, solar space and water heating is reasonably affordable and offers several options for boosting the energy efficiency of your home and reducing your carbon footprint—a calculation of the amount of greenhouse gases we produce, measured in units of carbon dioxide.

There are two main types of solar wall collectors. The distinction between them depends on how the heated air is circulated in the home. Thermosiphoning panels use natural convection to move warm air into the structure. Active solar wall collectors use

This is a retreat located in the Cascades Mountains of Washington State, designed by Davis Studio Architecture + Design. Solar space heating for the residence is provided by energy-efficient radiant heat under bamboo flooring.

a small fan, which circulates the air through the unit for superior heat gain. Using a thermostatically controlled blower unit can boost efficiency by as much as 50 percent, which can easily offset the cost in electricity to operate it. It is often possible to join your collector to existing ductwork and deliver heat to rooms of the home beyond where the collector interfaces with the wall. When planning on the kind of collector to install, it is vital to properly establish the system size you will require to heat the living space desired. Solar wall collectors can function well to condition a single room, several rooms, or even your entire home if it is sized correctly.

Sometimes small fans are added to circulate the heat, but moving parts and the use of outside power are generally minimized. In contrast to the passive systems discussed previously, active space heating systems depend on hardware like rooftop collectors to accumulate and circulate warm air. They employ air or a liquid heated by a solar collector, which is then delivered via fans, pumps, or thermosiphoning to a storage unit.

▲
When heated water circulates through tubes under the flooring, the floor warms up and the heat radiates throughout the home, providing an even, constant, comfortable heat.

Heat Quantity

Active solar heating systems are typically planned to supply as much as three-quarters of a home's heating needs. However, studies have shown that active space heating

Green Roofing

Increasingly, businesses and homeowners alike are discovering the joys of "green roofing"—covering their rooftop with a low-maintenance layer of soil and plant life. Green roofs reduce household cooling and heating expenses through shade and evaporation. Not only will they reduce noise levels in an urban home, the protection from the elements provided by a green roof can double the life of a home's underlying conventional roof. Green roofs also help with a host of urban environmental challenges by filtering storm water, alleviating flooding, cooling the surrounding air, and absorbing CO_2. Last but not least, they provide what city dwellers have known for centuries: a small green oasis offers a tremendous psychological benefit during the heat of summer.

This beautiful home has a unique feature that helps reduce heating and cooling expenses—a sod roof.

systems are most affordable when sized to handle about half of a household's heating needs. Systems designed to offer more are not cost effective because most of the excess capacity is only used on the coldest winter days, remaining unused the rest of the year.

If your system provides only 50 percent of your needs, then the rest has to be produced by a backup system—such as a conventional furnace or biomass stove. It should be noted that most building codes and mortgage lenders require a backup heating unit. To be safe, backup heating systems should be able to deliver all your home heat for stretches of overcast, when no solar heat is to be had.

Thermosiphoning Air Panels

A thermosiphoning air panel (TAP) is an additional economical solar collector that warms air through convection. TAP collectors are typically mounted against an exterior wall of the home. TAPs are constructed of a sheet of glazing mounted in a metal or wooden frame with an airspace and a dark, corrugated aluminum sheet behind it. Behind that plate lies an additional airspace, where heated air ascends and enters the house through a top vent. As the heated air exits the unit, cooler air is sucked into the front of the panel through a bottom vent at floor level.

Active Collectors

Experience has shown that one can get better heat output from a solar collector such as the thermosiphoning air panel by adding a blower or by increasing the size of the collector. A blower by itself can raise warm-air circulation as much as

▲ ▶

This remodel by Michael Heacock + Associates on the San Francisco Bay was designed with a high-efficiency water heater for radiant heat, which eliminates the need for forced-air vents.

20 percent, and the modest increase in electricity needed is compensated for by increased heating power. You also can augment the yield of solar collectors by expanding the size. One downside of both active and thermosiphoning collectors is that they need to be shaded in winter to avoid damaging the unit and creating excessive heat in the home.

Radiant Floor Systems

A method of heat delivery well suited to active solar systems is radiant floor heat. Radiant floor heating often utilizes copper pipes or plastic tubing in a concrete slab floor, and can function reasonably well even in frigid climates. When heated water circulates through the tubes, the floor warms up, and the heat radiates upward into the

The Stag's Leap Residence, located in Napa Valley, was designed by Backen Gillam Architects. The 3,000-square-foot home is situated on the banks of a private pond facing the Mayacama mountain range. The interior spaces are kept comfortable by a radiant floor system.

room. When correctly designed and installed, these systems are some of the most effective and cozy space heating systems on the market.

Adding It Up

With state incentives and tax credits, adding solar hot water and space heating can be extremely practical financially, with paybacks often in as little as four years. Retrofitting with solar hot water is typically more economical than installing solar space heating. However, in new construction, solar space heating systems can present considerable energy savings for many decades. Furthermore, solar-powered systems present financial advantages that cannot adequately be measured simply in terms of payback. Besides doing something positive for generations to come by using renewable energy, the money you save by installing a solar water or space heating system during home

Ground Source Heating

Ground source or geothermal heat pumps are a lesser known but rapidly emerging form of renewable home heating. Not to be confused with the geothermal heating in places such as Iceland that comes from naturally occurring underground steam, ground source heat pumps rely on pipes buried deep underground that use the earth's stable ground temperature (50 to 55 degrees Fahrenheit in most of the United States) to keep a home warm in winter and cool in summer. Ground source systems consume 25 to 50 percent less energy than conventional heating and cooling systems. The main downside is the up-front cost of the system and its installation, but a list of federal and state incentives can be found at the Geothermal Heat Pump Consortium Web site: www.geoexchange.com.

building or remodeling will, no doubt, quickly surpass the increase in your mortgage or home equity payment.

Biomass for Home Heating

Another form of solar energy in the form of what we call "sequestered sunshine" is biomass. Biomass is basically any form of renewable organic material that can be converted to energy. Biomass can easily be grown or harvested, used, and replaced. For the purposes of the homeowner, when speaking of biomass, we are talking about corn, wood, or biofuel burned for home heating.

Burning plant matter may not seem like the most environmentally friendly option for household heat, but the effective use of biomass releases considerably less CO_2 than fossil fuels and can play a vital part in reducing greenhouse gas emissions. This is because when energy crops are grown sustainably, their combustion releases basically the same level of CO_2 taken in during photosynthesis, with no net change in greenhouse gas levels.

Heat Output and Capacity—It is estimated that the average medium-size American home needs from 10,000 to 20,000 BTUs (British Thermal Units) of heat per hour. A biomass stove may easily heat a 3,000-square-foot house in Alabama but only a 1,500-square-foot house in New England, due to the different climate. Furthermore, an old wood-frame house might have double the heat loss of a new energy-efficient home of comparable size in the same region.

Woodstoves—There are many advantages of heating with wood, but the greatest benefit is perhaps the financial savings compared with the fossil fuel alternatives. Depending on where you live, and if you inhabit a well-insulated, moderately sized home, you may be able to heat your entire house with a single woodstove if it is correctly sized and properly located. The most successful wood heating is usually achieved

The woodstove in the living room of the Kingsley-Debenham Cottage in Portland, Oregon, offers a huge financial savings compared to fossil-fuel alternatives.

in homes with open floor plans, where the woodstove can be centrally located. Even with circulating fans, larger homes with many rooms and poorly sealed older homes have greater difficulty maintaining adequate even heat.

Pellet Stoves—Wood pellets are made primarily from waste wood products, such as residue of lumber mills and the wood-manufacturing industry, and other wood-fiber products. The raw material is ground and compressed into pellets. Once installed, pellet stoves are easy to maintain and much less labor intensive and dirty than traditional woodstoves. A pellet stove appears similar to a woodstove but has an automated auger to feed pellets from the hopper into the fire. Pellet stoves have high up-front costs of $3,000 or more but usually do not need special chimneys or insulated flues because there is such complete combustion that produces very little smoke—which makes them a great environmental choice.

These hardwood pellets are manufactured from waste-wood products and are used for burning in pellet stoves.

The cost for wood pellets ranges from $250 to $300 (fall 2007 prices) a ton. A general guideline from the industry is to expect to burn two pounds of pellets per hour at peak capacity. That is about half the cost of heating oil and equivalent to the expense of burning cordwood. Pellet fuel now has the flexibility of being burned in a freestanding pellet stove, a fireplace insert, or a high-capacity central furnace. One potential downside is that pellet stoves require electricity to operate their auger, but battery backups are available for most stoves in case the power goes out. Other downsides are the limited availability of pellets some stove owners face, particularly near the end of the heating season. Another issue is cost, as pellet prices have risen dramatically in recent years.

Corn and Switchgrass—In recent years there has been a rising interest in corn-burning stoves. Corn stoves have been on the market for nearly two decades but in fairly limited quantities. These are not significantly different from wood pellet stoves except they typically need a vent pipe specially designed for the higher heat of corn combustion. Corn fuel has become so well liked that several manufacturers and dealers have modified their stoves to burn both wood pellets and corn or a combination of these. A new entry on the market that shows great promise is clean-burning switchgrass—an easily renewable resource popular in South America but ideally suited for American farms. At one of our solar stores, we have had great success burning a combination of corn, wood pellets, and switchgrass pellets to ward off the Vermont winter chill.

This special low-moisture-content corn is burned in a household corn stove.

Masonry Heaters—Another form of biomass heat growing in popularity is the masonry heater, also called the Russian stove. This consists of a large central column of brick or stone that resembles a fireplace chimney in many ways. An enclosed wood box is connected to winding channels that allow for nearly total combustion. In addition to architectural beauty, these devices have several advantages, including terrific heat storage, a clean burn, and super efficiency. The biggest downside besides the labor involved in wood heating is the high initial cost.

Outdoor Boilers—In these systems, a metal shed-like structure sits outside the home. A large firebox is surrounded by a water jacket from which heated water is pumped underground to the house. These are best suited for remote rural sites, mainly when heating several buildings such as barns or workshops. Unfortunately, these are Environmental Protection Agency (EPA)–exempt because combustion is often poor; therefore, they are criticized for their heavy emissions.

Wood-Fired Central Heat—Central wood heaters and boilers distribute heat with forced hot air or circulating hot water systems. Because of their electric thermostats, pumps, and blowers, wood-fired central heaters require electricity to operate, so they are not as reliable as a woodstove if the power goes out. A reliable source of firewood is often not available outside of rural areas, and handling and burning wood is labor intensive and often dirty work too.

Biodiesel—Although biodiesel is usually thought of as the hot new fuel for diesel trucks and cars, it is just as well-suited as a fuel for oil-fired furnaces and boilers. There are even new woodstove-type heating options that burn biofuel instead of pellets or corn. Processed from new and recycled vegetable oil or animal fat, biodiesel fuel has the added quality of being biodegradable, nontoxic, and renewable. Indeed, biodiesel can be produced in only a few months; and, like wood, plants grown for biofuel only release the carbon dioxide absorbed during photosynthesis when burned. The major negatives to heating with biodiesel are availability and price. Finding a local source of biodiesel can be difficult as well, and locating a fuel oil dealer that offers biodiesel home deliveries can be even more challenging in most areas of the country. Additionally, biodiesel usually costs more than heating oil.

This Russian fireplace gives not only rustic charm but also considerable thermal mass and extremely efficient—and long lasting—wood heat.

6

Wind Power for the Home

Humans have long been harnessing the power of the wind, and wind energy is now the fastest-growing energy source on earth. A wind turbine is simply a device that converts the kinetic energy of wind into mechanical energy. If that energy is used directly by machinery, such as a water pump or grain mill, as a rule, the machine is referred to as a windmill. However, if that mechanical energy is then transformed into electricity, the device is more correctly termed a wind generator or wind turbine.

Contemporary home wind energy systems commonly consist of a rotor, a frame-mounted generator or alternator, a tail, a steel tower, electrical wiring, and what we call the "balance of system": its controllers, inverters, and batteries. Through its spinning rotors, the wind turbine catches the power of the wind and turns it into motion. As in solar power systems, small turbines can be set up to feed the electrical grid and charge battery banks to provide energy to off-grid homes, or both of these can be in grid-tied homes with battery backup.

Fixed, guyed towers do not need the open drop zone that tilt-up towers call for, but they still require open space for the guy wires.

Wind generators can be divided into two general categories based on the orientation of the turbine's axis on which the blades rotate. Generators that rotate around a horizontal axis are the most common and what we normally think of when we think of wind power. Vertical-axis generators are less frequently seen but are growing quickly in popularity, particularly in Europe.

Horizontal-Axis Wind Generators—Horizontal-axis wind generators are mounted at the top of a tower, and most are oriented into the wind by a simple tail-like fin, whereas large commercial turbines generally employ advanced wind sensors and motors to align themselves. Inside, gears convert the relatively slow movement of the blades into high rpm motion needed for generating sufficient levels of electricity.

Windmills for pumping water and generating electricity were once common across rural America before the electrification projects of the 1930s and 1940s.

The Growing Power of Wind Power

Critics often say large-scale wind energy is inconsistent, unattractive, hazardous to wildlife, and financially impractical. But larger, quieter, and more productive wind turbines are emerging across America. Some states, such as New York and California, require that utilities obtain a specific percentage of their electricity from wind. In 2007, Texas surpassed California in installed wind power capacity. The Lone Star State now has the potential to power more than half a million American homes. More than two-dozen states have wind farms capable of generating nearly ten gigawatts of electricity, more than enough to power two million homes, and at prices increasingly competitive with natural gas, nuclear power, and so-called "clean coal." The price of a kilowatt-hour of electricity generated by wind now averages about four cents, an 80 percent decrease from twenty-five years ago.

▶

A quarter of the U.S. population lives in areas potentially suitable for small-scale wind power.

Vertical-Axis Wind Generators—As you might imagine, vertical-axis wind generators have their rotor shaft running vertically. The benefits of this system is that they are placed closer to the ground, so a large tower is not required to support it, and it need not be actively oriented into the wind. The downside is that they are habitually affected by a stressful torqueing action as well as by a drag effect created when the vertical blades rotate into the wind. It can also be difficult to mount vertical-axis turbines on towers to capture greater wind speeds, requiring that they function in the turbulent, weaker wind currents near the ground, which translates to lower energy production.

Swept Area and Wind Speed

Energy generation from wind turbines is influenced by two primary factors: rotor diameter and wind speed. Simply put, the more area the rotor blades cover, the more energy you will capture. The speed and volume of the wind you can capture at your site are the best gauges of your potential electrical output. Since wind power is relative to wind speed cubed, minute variances in average wind speed represent immense boosts in accessible wind power. Wind experts are quick to point out, however, that ground clutter and natural features at your site such as trees, your own home, and hillsides all increase turbulence and decrease wind speed. This deprives a wind generator of potential energy and must be taken into account when installing a home-sized wind system.

Evaluating Wind Energy at Your Site

A wind generator big enough to supply a worthwhile part of the electricity considered necessary for a typical American home is estimated to need at least one acre of property. Fortunately, more than a quarter of homes in this country sit on sites appropriate to harvesting small-scale wind energy. As with solar power, wind systems frequently have high initial costs but modest or no operating expense for the remainder of the system's twenty- to thirty-year life. The practicality of a micro wind system depends on several factors, such as the existing wind at your location sufficient to cover your energy requirements, regulatory or zoning ordinances that bar setting up a wind turbine in your neighborhood, rebates and incentives available, and whether your investment's payback justifies the expense.

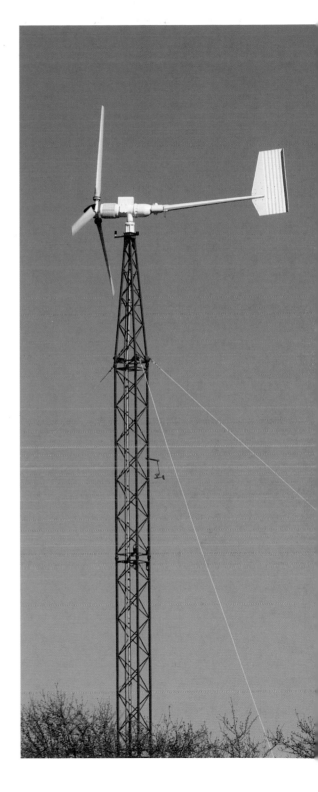

The NowHouse is a modular single-family home assembled for display in parking lot A of the Pac Bell Park. It was designed by architect Toby Long and built by Clever Homes. The home was originally meant to be auctioned for sale on eBay but was eventually donated to the city of San Francisco. An energy-saving plus for this beautiful home is that it has wind energy capability.

The good news is that wind power can be one of the most financially sensible, sustainable energy systems a homeowner can buy. Depending on the available wind at your homesite, a micro wind power system can cut your utility expenses from 50 to 90 percent, eliminate the need to string power lines to new homes and remote sites, avert power outages, and cut your contribution to greenhouse gases.

If the wind blows regularly at your location, a small-scale wind energy system is probably a good investment. First, you need to research your annual wind speeds and the prevailing direction of the wind where you live. If you live in varied terrain with lots of trees, hills, or rocky outcroppings, you have to select the installation site carefully to avoid sheltered or highly turbulent areas. Ideally, the turbine should be situated upwind of houses and trees, and a minimum of thirty feet above anything within one hundred yards of the tower.

Another way to judge the wind resource is to obtain average wind speed information from a local airport. However, be aware that local terrain differences and other factors might cause the wind speed supplied by your airport to be different from your particular location, and bear in mind that airport wind speed is generally measured at only twenty to thirty feet above the ground. Since average wind speed increases with height, your wind speed atop a hundred-foot tower could be more than 25 percent greater. The National Climatic Data Center gathers this data from airports across the

A cutting-edge vertical access wind turbine.

It is often wise to supplement wind power with solar or hydropower for consistent power production.

country and offers wind information for sale, but your renewable energy retailer or installer should give you a wind resource report based on geological and satellite data as part of your system design and installation plan.

Wind resource maps online also can be utilized for estimating the wind resource in your location. Usually, the highest average annual wind speeds in this country are found near the seashore, on ridgelines, and in the Midwest. However, countless areas have winds powerful enough to power a micro wind generator. More detailed wind resource information, including the summaries of wind data from approximately 1,000 airports, is available in the Wind Energy Resource Atlas of the United States, published by the U.S. Department of Energy, and can be found at the National Wind Technology Center Web site (www.nrel.gov/wind/) and the Department of Energy's Wind Powering America Web site (www.windpoweringamerica.gov).

Whether your system is grid tied or stand alone, you must also factor in the distance between the wind generator and your house (the wire run) since a considerable amount of electricity may be lost in transit if the distance is too great. Installing greater lengths of wire or larger gauge wire also raises your system price. Because wire run losses are smaller with alternating current (AC) as compared to direct current (DC), if you have a lengthy wire run, it is prudent to invert DC to AC.

Local Regulations

When considering potential sites for your wind turbine, be certain to verify land use laws, zoning regulations, and building codes for ordinances that might affect installation of a wind turbine on your property. Many locales restrict tower height or require a clear zone around your tower in case it falls over (this rarely happens). Despite the fact that wind turbines are vastly more visually pleasing than power lines, generally unfounded complaints about noise, wildlife impact, and aesthetics are raised regarding wind turbines by communities more than against any other renewable energy system, so be prepared. Nevertheless, wind power is gaining acceptance rapidly as we enter what promises to be a golden age of green power, so it is getting easier for renewable energy pioneers every day.

Wind turbines should be installed at least 30 feet above any turbulence-producing obstructions within 300 feet of the tower.

Wind energy is now the fastest-growing energy source on earth.

Turbine Sizing

The size of the wind turbine your home requires depends on how you plan to use it. A typical home uses approximately 10,000 to 12,000 kilowatt hours of electricity annually. Depending on the wind resource at your site, you would need an expensive five- to fifteen-kilowatt-hour turbine to meet this demand. Conversely, a more economical one-kilowatt-hour wind turbine might be sufficient to cover the requirements of a household needing 250 to 300 kilowatt hours per month at a site with an annual average wind speed of fourteen miles per hour or better. Manufacturers and installers will give you the expected annual energy output of the turbines they sell according to your annual average wind speed.

Towers

Wind-energy experts will always tell you that the higher you go, the better the wind. Because wind speeds increase with height over level ground, wind turbines are erected atop a tower. In essence, the greater the height of your tower, the more power your wind

Humans have used wind power for centuries, but after decades of being forgotten, wind is now seeing a dramatic resurgence worldwide.

turbine can generate. The tower also lifts the turbine above air turbulence at ground level. A common maxim is to mount the wind turbine on a tower so that the tips of the rotor blades are a minimum of thirty feet above any obstacle that is within 300 feet.

Experiments have demonstrated that fairly small increases in tower height can give higher rates of power production more than enough to justify the added cost. For instance, to raise a ten-kilowatt-hour turbine from a sixty-foot tower to a one-hundred-foot tower produces a 10 percent increase in system cost but will produce about 25 percent more energy. Mounting turbines on rooftops is not recommended because wind turbines vibrate and therefore transmit that vibration to the structure on which they are mounted. This can lead to annoying noise levels and structural damage to the building, and roofs can create excessive turbulence that can shorten the life of the turbine and limit its effectiveness.

The three basic tower types are tilt-up towers, fixed towers, and freestanding towers:

Tilt-Up Towers—Although tilt-up towers are more costly, these give the homeowner a painless way to perform repairs on micro turbines of five kilowatts or smaller. Moreover, you or your installer will never have to climb the tower, and if there are mechanical issues with the turbine, you can generally lower it in less than an hour and raise it again just as quickly once repairs are complete. The major downside of tilt-up towers is the footprint required since you need an open area for the tower to lie down.

Fixed, Guyed Towers—A fixed, guyed tower is erected once and does not tilt down again. Guy wires hold it in place, and any maintenance is done by climbing the tower. Fixed, guyed towers do not need the open drop zone that a tilt-up tower needs, but you still must have open space for the guy wires. Costs for these are comparable to tilt-up towers, but they can be installed on many sites that will not accommodate a tilt-up tower because they don't need as much cleared level space.

Freestanding Towers—If aesthetics, not cost, are a primary concern, a freestanding tower might be your first choice. There are no guy wires, no tilting involved, and free-standing towers only need a modest space for the tower base. Freestanding towers take two basic forms. Both types are usually assembled on the ground and lifted with a crane. The most common version is the three-legged style, with tubular legs connected by angle iron braces. The other option is a monopole tower—a single tube similar to what is used for utility-scale wind turbines, only smaller. These are often quite expensive and are out of reach financially for most small-scale renewable energy users. A freestanding tower will cost at least one-third to one-half more than a tilt-up or fixed, guyed tower.

Balance of System

The balance of system parts that you need in addition to the turbine and the tower depends on your application. Most manufacturers and dealers will provide you with a system package that includes all the components you need for your application. The balance of system required will also depend on whether the system is grid connected, stand alone, or part of a hybrid system. For a residential grid-connected application, the balance of system parts may include a controller, storage batteries, inverter, and wiring.

▲
A less-common two-bladed horizontal-access turbine.

▶

Wind turbines should not be installed on rooftops or attached to buildings where vibrations can cause undesirable noise or structural damage.

▶

This is a modern version of the eggbeater-style "Darrieus" vertical-axis wind turbine developed by French inventor Georges Jean Marie Darrieus in the 1920s.

Cost

Installation costs vary greatly depending on local zoning, permits, and utility interconnection costs. A small turbine can cost anywhere from less than $1,000 for small "camp" sizes to $50,000 for large home systems, depending on size, application, and service agreements with the manufacturer. The American Wind Energy Association (AWEA) estimates that a ten-kilowatt home wind system costs approximately $32,000 compared to a similar photovoltaic solar energy system that would cost over $80,000. Wind energy becomes more cost-effective as the size of the turbine's rotor increases. Although small turbines cost less in initial outlay, they are proportionally more expensive.

The cost of an installed residential wind energy system with an eighty-foot tower, batteries, and inverter typically ranges from $15,000 to $50,000 for a three- to ten-kilowatt system. Although wind energy systems involve a significant initial investment, they can be competitive with conventional energy sources when you account for a lifetime of reduced or avoided utility costs. The length of the payback period—the time before the savings resulting from your system equals the cost of the system itself—depends on the system you choose, the wind resource on your site, electricity costs in your area, and how your wind system is used. For example, if you live in California and have received the 50 percent rebate of your small wind system, and if you have net metering and an average annual wind speed of fifteen miles per hour at your site, your simple payback would be approximately six years.

The Bottom Line

The Wind Energy Payback Period Workbook found at www.nrel.gov/wind/docs/ is a spreadsheet tool that can help you analyze the economics of a small-wind electric system and decide whether wind energy will work for you. It asks you to provide information about how you are going to finance the system, the characteristics of your location, and the properties of the system you are considering. It then provides you with a payback estimate measured in years. If it takes too long to recoup your investment—i.e., the number of years for payback exceeds the life of the system—wind energy may not be desirable for you.

Micro-Hydro Power

Micro-hydro power is a form of renewable energy where the energy of falling water is harnessed to produce electricity. Micro-hydro is often the cheapest form of renewable energy available to the homeowner in terms of kilowatt-hours of electricity produced.

All hydroelectric systems convert the energy of flowing water into electrical energy. Definitions vary by country, but micro-hydroelectric systems are generally thought of as generating 300 kilowatts of peak power or less. These small-scale systems can be adopted by homeowners with modest environmental impact since most micro-hydro systems draw power from a waterway with minimal change in the water flow. Distinct from commercial hydroelectric plants, micro-hydroelectric systems use very small weirs or dams, which hold back very little water. In addition, because only small diversion dams or intakes are needed for micro-hydroelectric systems, they rarely influence migratory habits of fish or the waterway's ecology.

As with wind, water has provided civilization with a reliable power source for centuries.

Basically, micro-hydroelectric systems convert the energy of moving water to electrical energy. The energy created is sustainable and the practice does not generate greenhouse gases. Domestic micro-hydro used in off-grid applications can be direct current (DC) systems for charging batteries, or grid-tied alternating current (AC) systems. In all micro-hydro systems, water turns a wheel or a propeller-like device to spin a turbine and generate electricity.

Water power is measured as the combination of "flow" and "head." Both must exist in sufficient amounts to create electricity. Water is diverted from a flowing source into a pipeline, where it is directed downhill and through the turbine. This is the flow. The vertical drop, or head, creates pressure at the bottom end of the pipeline. This pressurized water emerging from the end of the pipe creates the force that drives the turbine. Added flow or head produces more electricity. A little loss in power can be expected as the energy in the flowing water is transformed into electrical power, but this can be reduced by a well-designed system. Every facet of your hydroelectric system, from water intake to turbine-generator configuration to wire length and gauge, will influence its effectiveness. Turbine choice is particularly vital and has to be suited to your stream's flow and head for optimum efficiency.

Micro-Hydro Advantages

There are many advantages to micro-hydro power besides being an efficient and renewable energy resource. Micro-hydro requires relatively little flow and head to produce electricity. In addition, it generates a more reliable supply of electricity when compared to other home-sized renewable energy systems. Another advantage is that its peak energy period is in winter, when greater levels of electricity are generally needed and solar power is diminished. Micro-hydro power, unlike large-scale hydroelectric plants, is considered a very environmentally friendly choice because of its minute effect on the ecosystem—water passes through the system and back into the river or stream with little or no impact on the waterway. Finally, micro-hydroelectric is perhaps the most cost-effective energy option with costs for a small system ranging from as little as $1,000 to $20,000, depending on your power needs and your site's location.

The Trout Farm Residence in Santa Margarita, California, was renovated by the San Luis Sustainability Group and has hydroelectric on-site generation.

Micro-Hydro Disadvantages

Micro-hydro has many advantages over conventional grid power as well as over solar and wind power, but it does have a few disadvantages to consider. Not everyone has a suitable site—a reliable, year-round water source is needed. Other aspects to think about are the remoteness of the power source from the home as well as the quality of your water source. Another disadvantage is that unlike solar and wind systems, where you can add modules or a larger turbine, you probably cannot increase the energy potential of your water source, so scalability is limited. Another problem, if you need lots of power for cooling, is the natural reduction of potential energy output in the summertime in many regions, when energy demand peaks. Lastly, although environmental impact is minimal, you may encounter an added layer of regulatory bureaucracy to obtain the permits you need to draw power from a river or stream.

Evaluating Your Water Resource

If you have an appropriate site, exploiting the embodied energy in a stream or river can be the most cost-effective way to make renewable electricity. In comparison to the changeability of solar and wind power, a waterway's flow is reasonably constant, making micro-hydro systems perhaps the most dependable of all the green power choices. However, micro-hydro has very strict site requirements. Sadly, many homeowners think they have a great water resource but it turns out, for a variety of reasons, to be insufficient or impractical for micro-hydro power.

There are some primary issues influencing whether you have a suitable micro-hydro location. As with other forms of renewable energy discussed previously, the initial step is to establish the quantity of electricity you need to generate. This requires calculating how much power your family consumes and if you can improve your conservation and efficiency. You can switch from electricity to another fuel. Your next move is to establish the vertical drop of the falling water from the likely intake location to where the turbine will be situated. The distance between the intake and turbine is also vital to know. Then, you must measure the flow in the waterway during different seasons. If you want the system to produce year-round energy, the minimum flow

The electric energy created by the flowing water on this site is the cheapest form of renewable energy available in terms of kilowatt-hours of electricity produced.

must be calculated during the dry days of late summer, when you have had several rain-free days.

Micro-hydro power works best in locations where the water source is constantly flowing, and where you can produce a minimum of 100 watts of continuous power. If the supply varies dramatically with the seasons, it could still be worthwhile to invest in micro-hydro, depending on whether your energy production in peak times offsets your installation cost. Grid power, other renewable energy systems, or a backup generator will be needed, however, when your water is not flowing adequately.

This stream is more than adequate for micro-hydro power.

System Components

An intake collects the water and a pipeline delivers it to the turbine, which converts the water's energy into mechanical shaft power. The turbine drives the generator that then converts shaft power into electricity. In an AC system, this power goes directly to the loads. In a battery-based system, the power is stored in batteries, which feed the loads as needed. Controllers may be required to regulate the system. Like other renewable energy systems discussed earlier, a micro-hydro system consists of linked components. Water flows into the intake of the system, and electrical power emerges at your home. Along the way, there are numerous devices that help the system run effectively. Below is a brief summary of micro-hydro components.

Turbines—There are two types of micro-hydro turbines: impulse and reaction.

Impulse turbine wheels spin freely out of the water. Water is channeled onto the turbine wheel (the runner) by nozzles. Impulse turbines are usually installed on sites with heads greater than thirty feet and are the most widespread type of turbine seen in domestic micro-hydro systems. Impulse turbine types are pelton, turgo, and cross flow.

Reaction turbine runners, on the other hand, spin submerged underwater in a sealed container. These less common turbines are typically installed in low-head situations. In reaction turbines, the energy of water pressure is converted to speed inside the sealed container. They spin around in "reaction" to the action of water squirting from jets in the arms of its rotor, much like the action of a rotating lawn sprinkler. Reaction turbine types are propeller and Francis.

Pipelines—The pipeline, or penstock, directs water into your turbine and provides the area that creates head pressure along the vertical drop. Basically, the pipeline takes the energy that is spread across the water source and focuses it on the turbine. Micro-hydro systems, with the exception of propeller machines with open intakes, need a pipe to channel water to the turbine. Water first passes through a screen or filter to stop sediment and debris that might block or damage the turbine. Pipelines are usually plastic, but steel or concrete ones are also used. Pipe diameter, length, material, and routing all have an effect on efficiency.

Intakes—The intake is characteristically the uppermost end of your micro-hydro system, where the water is diverted from the source into a pipe that feeds the turbine. An intake can be as rudimentary as a pipe fitted with a filtering screen in a pool of water, or as complicated as a dam blocking a stream or river. Water-diversion systems serve a couple of functions. The primary function is to afford a deep enough pool to form a turbulence-free inlet for your pipe. The other purpose is to keep debris from entering the pipeline.

Batteries

Lead-acid deep-cycle batteries are generally the type used in micro-hydro systems. Deep-cycle batteries are intended to endure the repeated charging and discharging common in renewable energy systems. However, unlike household nicad batteries, which can be completely drained without negative results, lead-acid batteries should never be fully discharged. Unlike PV and wind-power systems, micro-hydro systems need, at most, only a day or two of battery storage because of the fairly constant flow of water. An added bonus is that since the batteries used in a micro-hydro system are discharged less frequently, they last longer than those in other green power applications.

Controllers

Micro-hydro systems, like other renewable energy systems with a battery storage bank, need overcharge and overdischarge protection. Charge controllers redirect the power to diversion load when battery voltage peaks, guarding the system's generator from an over-speed or overvoltage state. Overdischarge controls cut off the power coming from the batteries when their voltage falls too low. Several inverters have this low-voltage shutoff capability built in. Numerous monitoring devices such as volt meters and amp-hour meters are also available and should be seriously considered as protection for your investment.

Take a Green Homes Tour

Despite its name, the National Solar Tour showcases more than just solar power; it also has a whole range of renewable and energy-efficient technologies in homes across America. The tours demonstrate to those interested in green energy how average homeowners get their power needs from the sun, wind, micro-hydro, and other sustainable resources. A growing facet of the tours is conserving energy through green building design, energy-efficient appliances, and sustainable building materials. National Solar Tour attendees learn firsthand from homeowners how their green energy choices protect against power blackouts, improve energy independence, and reduce their carbon footprint. Many homeowners offer participants what amounts to a virtual crash course in incentives and payback cycles of energy efficiency and renewable energy solutions. Tours are put on by American Solar Energy Society chapters, state energy offices, environmental and conservation organizations, renewable energy businesses, and volunteers. The National Solar Tour is held on the first Saturday of each October, National Energy Awareness Month. For more information, check out the ASES Web site: www.ases.org.

The "powerhouse" is a simple box that encloses the turbine, generator, and controls, and protects them from the harsh environment of the waterway.

Cost

Micro-hydro power, in the right location and near a dependable water source, can cost the homeowner as much as 90 percent less than a photovoltaic system of equivalent yield. Because of the steady level of power, micro-hydro users can more easily use high-wattage kitchen appliances and space heaters that can cause problems for the off-grid solar electric system owner. Micro-hydro systems suitable for the average family of four can be installed for $2,000 to $5,000 per peak kilowatt capacity—considerably less than solar and wind power—depending on the site and the water source. Low-head applications that need a high flow rate are more costly than high-head applications because they demand bigger, more expensive components. Conversely, high-head low-flow systems are the cheapest. Because system equipment costs are lower and the watt-per-dollar return is higher than for other renewable systems, micro-hydro is a fantastic green energy option for the lucky few with an appropriate site.

8

Financing, Incentives, Rebates, and Tax Credits

There has never been a better time to invest in renewable energy. One of the greatest forces behind the burgeoning popularity of green power is the availability of liberal financial incentives. As a matter of fact, incentives now equal more than $3 billion for household sustainable energy systems. In many states, rebate programs refund more than half of the homeowner's cost. Additionally, several states offer tax credits, exemptions, and low-interest loans to sweeten the deal.

Installing renewable energy systems on a home can provide considerable tax advantages. The Energy Policy Act provides a 30 percent federal tax credit of up to $2,000 for residential photovoltaic and solar domestic hot water equipment.

Financing

As we have shown previously, renewable energy systems often require a sizeable capital investment. Thankfully, if a homeowner does not wish to pay for their renewable home energy system out of pocket, there are now a host of financing alternatives for green energy that were not available just a few short years ago. Your renewable energy retailer can be an incredibly valuable resource in discovering financing options available in your state and which are the most appropriate for you. By financing your renewable energy system, you can spread the cost over many years, and the interest payments are often deductible. Typical financing options include unsecured loans, home equity loans, and home refinancing. Consult your financial institution about these options, and see the resources section at the end of this book for more information.

A Final Word on System Costs

Without a doubt, the question we get more than any other at USA Solar Store is "What does a solar-electric system cost for an average home?" Justifiably, our potential customers want a ballpark price of our solar, wind, and micro-hydro systems so they can judge whether they feel it is worth it or simply whether they can afford it. Often, they will go away for a year or more and come back when they have made up their mind or saved up the money, and we respect that. Unfortunately, we are often unable to give a simple answer to that question because there are so many factors involved.

As stated before, the average American home uses 800 to 1,000 kilowatt hours of electricity every month. However, estimating system costs solely on that figure alone might produce a misleading answer. Power consumption often varies significantly, depending on the time of year, the age and type of appliances used most, and your lifestyle habits in general. At the risk of sounding too repetitive, follow the advice in the Energy Conservation chapter because this information will greatly influence the amount you will end up spending on a renewable energy system. Again, every dollar spent on improving energy efficiency lowers the system cost fourfold. Adding to the complexity of determining cost is the tremendous difference between the square footage of homes (and how much is actually used) and personal energy consumption throughout the different stages of life and among occupants.

In net metering, the homeowner is charged for the electricity bought from the power company minus the electricity generated by their renewable energy system. The meter spins forward, as usual, when energy flows from the grid into the home, and backward when current flows from the building to the utility.

Net Metering

According to the federal Public Utility Regulatory Policies Act, power companies must allow you to connect your electrical energy system to the grid, and they are also obliged to purchase any surplus power you produce net of what you consume. In about three dozen states, renewable energy system owners profit from regulations governing net meter reading. In essence, the homeowner is charged for the electricity bought from the power company, minus the electricity generated by their renewable energy system. The meter spins forward as normal when energy flows from the grid into the home and backward when current flows from the building to the utility. With a net metering agreement, the homeowner is compensated at the retail electricity rate for kilowatt-hours of sustainable electricity transmitted to the utility. Net metering benefits are particularly important in regions with high electric rates. The local power company and the community in general benefit from reduced demand and the periods of peak demand, such as midday in summer, when renewable energy systems are at their most productive. In addition, many utilities also sell or trade energy credits based on their customers' production of power.

Net metering differs state to state and among utilities, but all net metering programs must detail their method of determining "net excess generation"—how the customer is compensated for electricity and the time period allowed to take the credit. If your net metering agreement measures net excess generation monthly, you may receive credit for the excess energy produced in that month only. A better deal is if your net metering regulations permit annual net excess generation in which the credit can be banked in your account for a year.

When a local utility does not have net metering, it usually requires the homeowner to install two meters: one to gauge the power you are taking from them and another to calculate the electricity you are sending out to the grid. Under these circumstances, the power company pays only the wholesale rate for the electricity you provide to them. This less-than-ideal arrangement should be taken into account when designing your system to avoid generating too much extra power or having to buy too much from the utility.

Power companies are required by the federal Public Utility Regulatory Policies Act to allow homeowners to connect their renewable energy system to the electrical grid. They must purchase any surplus power produced.

Rebates and State Tax Credits

There are many states and even some power companies offering credits that can off-set much of the cost for your solar array and components. These rebates or tax cred-its can aid in reducing system cost, but don't be tempted to buy a renewable energy system just to get these credits as many did in the 1970s—it is no longer worth it for those reasons alone. Most residential solar rebate programs are capped at a specific dollar amount, often equaling about 20 to 30 percent of per-watt cost. Tax incentives often feature a sales tax exemption for renewable energy systems, property tax exemptions, or state income tax credits, providing homeowners with a greatly reduced up-front cost. The National Database of State Incentives for Renewable Energy, listed in the resources section, features information on virtually every renewable energy incentive.

Federal Solar Tax Credit

In 2005, the Energy Policy Act established a 30 percent federal tax credit of up to $2,000 for pur-chasing and installing residential PV and solar domestic hot water equipment. Nearly all expenses, including labor for site preparation, assembly, and original installation, as well as for pipes and wires to connect the system to the home, are allowable. The system only has to be sited at a residence occupied by the taxpayer. This credit is subtracted from any federal taxes you owe, and as a credit, any excess comes back to you as a refund. Eligibility requirements state that components must be placed in service before December 31, 2008, but this has been extended in the past and likely will be again.

Solar Financing Options

As with any major home improvement, you can often finance a solar system with a home equity loan, which is generally repayable over a ten- to fifteen-year period and have interest rates much lower than many other types of loans. With a new home, you can simply fold the cost of a solar system into your mortgage. If you are purchasing or refinancing your house with an FHA loan, you can often increase that loan by 20 percent if the home has or will have a solar system. Many states, towns, and even some PV dealers also have attractive loan programs, so shop around.

9

System Design and Installation

Given enough research, and if you have enough experience with plumbing or wiring, you may very well be able to install your own renewable energy system. But chances are that you will need at least a little help from a professional installer. In this chapter we offer you a basic primer on what to know and how to happily negotiate your way through a successful green energy installation.

Before we go any farther, we need to address the issue of renewable energy systems available through mail order or on the Web. You will no doubt see some terrific prices on equipment on the Internet, but remember that things that seem too good to be true often are. Few mail-order dealers, with the exception of well-established companies such as Real Goods or Backwoods Solar, seldom can counsel you on system design or help you sort through and match the dizzying array of modules, inverters, charge controllers, and meters available these days. We have had countless people come into our stores hoping we can help them fix broken, mismatched, or improperly sized components. We frequently also hear of the old bait and switch, where the bargain-priced,

Solar panels last a very long time. The oldest residential modules are still functioning perfectly after thirty years. Nearly all solar modules now feature fifteen- to twenty-five-year warranties, reflecting the widespread industry confidence in their longevity.

high-quality products are always out of stock and people are pressured to accept inferior or malfunctioning products.

Comparing Solar, Wind, and Micro-Hydro

Weighing various green energy systems will depend on your homesite and what it supports. If you have great solar access, then photovoltaic might be your best choice. If you have reliable wind resources averaging nine miles per hour or more, then perhaps wind power should be your first option. If you have a reliable year-round source of running water, you are very fortunate and should give serious thought to a micro-hydro system. To gauge which system or combination of systems is right for you, read our previous chapters on the wide range of home energy options to judge what fits your conditions best, and consult the resources section for further in-depth reading and sources of information.

Hybrid Systems

What we have found over the years through experience, and most experts agree on this, is that hybrid systems that can use a combination of solar, wind, and/or running water are the most desirable, as one is often available when the other is not. For example, in summer, when the winds are calmer, there is usually more sun. Likewise, in early spring there is often heavy water flow in streams and rivers when the skies are overcast, winds are spotty, and PV typically underproduces. In reality, the most successful renewable energy systems are hybrids in that they use the electrical grid or a generator for backup power.

Professional Load Analysis and Site Surveys

A professional load analysis, like an energy audit, details your home-power consumption and offers you the most effective ways to lower your costs. Site surveys, on the other hand, are meant to evaluate your potential renewable energy resources. After these steps are taken, you are ready to design a green energy system that not only fits your family's unique energy requirements but also gives you the greatest benefit for your investment. Taking the time to do this extra work will

A good renewable energy retailer-installer will keep any negative visual impacts of your system to a minimum and help you navigate zoning and homeowner association hurdles in strictly regulated communities.

Renewable energy systems are ideal for this remote vacation retreat and in locations where bringing in utility services is difficult or prohibitively expensive.

no doubt lead to a more trouble-free installation as well as fewer unwanted costs and headaches down the road.

After the load analysis or energy audit, we and most other renewable energy retailers are able to start calculating what your system might cost and for which incentives and rebates you qualify. A general estimate of system size and the components required can be put together and then you will get an approximation of the price. We and many other renewable energy dealers also insist on a site survey before doing an estimate to avoid any misunderstandings. On more than one occasion, we have gone out to a property to begin planning a PV system, only to discover that the homeowner has absolutely no sun exposure and is unwilling to cut down a single tree to make it work.

If the homeowners decide not to go ahead with their green energy project, they will not have invested much at this point, only a few hundred dollars at most, and can walk

A combination of solar and wind can provide energy coverage in a multitude of conditions.

away easily. However, if the decision is made to move ahead with the system, the retailer will perform a site visit, if they have not already done so, to evaluate what green energy potential exists on the property. Site surveys cost anywhere from $50 to a few hundred dollars, but this investment will spare you from making bad decisions and unnecessary spending. Particularly in regard to long-term investments such as these, careful planning and design have a huge impact on system performance and on recouping your expenses more quickly.

Another situation we sometimes face as retailers is the customer who approaches us with a set-in-stone idea of what he or she wants. It may be that they saw PV modules on a nice home and liked the way they looked or they have been captivated by windmills since childhood and simply must have one. It is often difficult to talk these people out of their choices when it becomes obvious that their site is not suited to their green energy dreams. Stay open to suggestions from your retailer, trust what he says, but be wary of ones that give you overly optimistic projections—such as "you don't need to conserve or increase efficiency." There are certainly dealers out there more than happy to sell you a $70,000 system on which you could have spent much less.

Solar modules can be easily and attractively mounted to almost any roof style. A typical residential installation can take as little as a few days.

The Forest Stewardship Council

The Forest Stewardship Council (FSC) is an international organization promoting sustainably managed forests. The FSC sets international standards for responsible forest management and accredits third-party organizations that certify forest managers and forest product producers to FSC standards worldwide. The FSC label identifies products supporting sustainable forestry.

Insurance, Inspections, and Permits

In the majority of states, you have a legal right to install a renewable energy system on your property. Nevertheless, you will need to obtain permits from your city or county building department or perhaps even approval from a local homeowners association. Almost certainly you will be required to obtain a building permit and an electrical permit before installing a solar or wind energy system. Normally, your renewable energy dealer is responsible for this as part of your overall system package. However, make sure you have it in writing from your retailer if this is included. Be prepared to work closely with your green energy provider on these and other issues—especially in dealing with local governments with no experience in renewable energy installations.

There are currently clear national standards for connecting a home PV or wind system to the utility, and federal law requires the power company to provide you with an agreement to do so. These interconnection standards ensure that your system components are safely connected to the utility grid, for your sake as well as that of the power crew. If you tie your system to the utility grid, an interconnection agreement is mandatory. These interconnection agreements lay out the minimum insurance requirements, but for most homeowners, your existing homeowner's insurance policy more often than not adequately covers these.

In addition to your interconnection agreement spelling out the stipulations for connecting to the utility grid, the power company should provide you with a purchase and sale agreement detailing your net metering provisions, the payment schedule for power you produce, and other particulars.

Legal and Environmental Hurdles

Prior to investing lots of time and money, research (or have your renewable energy retailer research) any possible legal and environmental issues of installing a system at your property. This is especially true with wind power. Some communities limit the height of the structures allowed in residential zones, and local residents might object to wind systems blocking their view. No doubt you will encounter unfounded concerns about noise generated by your turbine or negative impacts on birds. These objections can often be overcome easily by providing the real facts about the low impact of renewable energy in a calm and courteous matter.

If your turbine will be grid tied, investigate beforehand the requirements for interconnection to the utility, and talk to other homeowners in your area with grid-connected renewable energy systems. Community zoning restrictions are available from local building inspectors and planning boards, which can inform you of the need for a building permit as well as supply a list of other requirements.

Going the DIY Route

Deciding to install your own renewable energy system is a choice that many homeowners make, but it should be done only after careful consideration. DIY can indeed slash as much as 25 percent of the total purchase price, but properly designing and installing a safe and reliable system is not a weekend remodeling project for the typical homeowner. Renewable energy installations (especially grid-tied ones) are very specialized, even if you are highly skilled at plumbing and wiring, and require lots of time and study of the system components and how they work together. That being said, there are a wealth of technical books and online resources available to educate you—many of them can be found in our resources section at the end of this book. However, most grid-tied systems are installed by licensed contractors with years of experience in designing safe, efficient systems. In addition, many state rebate programs demand that the installation is done by a licensed professional—so the money you save with DIY is often less than that lost in rebates and incentives.

Many installations require extensive site work before installation, so make sure to use licensed and experienced installers. FindSolar.com is a terrific resource to locate a solar pro.

Even for renewable energy customers who can perform much of their own installation, we usually recommend that the homeowner hire an electrician to finish—or at least check—all the electrical connections. It also should be noted that some components often require calibration or fine tuning once they are installed to achieve maximum performance, and this can be tricky even with an owner's manual and customer support.

Choosing an Installer

The company that sold you your system should ideally perform the installation or, at a minimum, provide you with a list of reputable installers. Failing that, solar and wind turbine manufacturers, state energy offices, or even your power company can offer installer contacts in your area if you purchased your components by mail order or on the Web. In many areas, renewable energy dealers and installers can also be found in the yellow pages. Your local Chamber of Commerce and the Better Business Bureau are also valuable sources of information. Last but not least, to find an installer in your area, ask your local American Solar Energy Society (ASES). The ASES has chapters in more than thirty states and can provide you with a comprehensive list of installers and dealers. Also check the ASES Find Solar Web site at www.findsolar.com, which lists solar professionals in North America.

A Last Word

One of the best resources in finding reputable dealers and installers is through other green energy users. Ask other homeowners with renewable energy systems in your area who they used and if they were happy with the service they received. Above all,

The U.S. Green Building Council

The U.S. Green Building Council (USGBC) is a nonprofit organization that promotes green building practices. Its Leadership in Energy and Environmental Design (LEED) Green Building Rating System rates high-performance sustainable buildings. Covering all building types, it emphasizes state-of-the-art strategies in sustainable site development, water conservation, energy efficiency, materials and resources selection, and indoor environmental quality.

A well-trained installer will ensure that you have the best type of inverter for your system.

when you talk to prospective installers, find out what services they provide, get references, and check those references carefully. Check with a minimum of an installer's three most recent customers. If you can, ask to visit some of the homes and speak with the homeowners. In some areas of the country, organizations such as the Northeast Sustainable Energy Association offer yearly "Solar Home Tours," where you can wander through some of America's best green homes and pick the brains of people living with renewable energy on a daily basis. The infectious enthusiasm of these folks goes a long way in relieving any jitters about making such a bold choice in your own life. This level of effort may seem rather time consuming, but it is well worth it—and it is a great way to catch the green energy bug!

Resources

Architects, Builders, and Designers

Allen Associates
835 North Milpas Street, Suite D
Santa Barbara, CA 93103
805.884.8777
www.dennisallenassociates.com

Campanelli Construction
809 Bond Avenue, #B
Santa Barbara, CA 93103
805.965.2883

Carol Venolia
www.naturalremodeling.com

Clever Homes, LLC
665 Third Street
San Francisco, CA 94107
415.344.0806
www.cleverhomes.net

Creative Spaces
401.398.2586

Davis Studio Architecture + Design
13105 Venice Boulevard
Los Angeles, CA 90066
310.572.6055
www.davisstudioad.com

Drew Maran
Drew Maran Construction, Inc.
480 Lytton Avenue, Suite 6
Palo Alto, CA 94301
650.323.8541
www.drewmaran.com

Green Hammer Construction
1323 SE 6th Avenue
Portland, OR 97214
503.804.1746
www.greenhammer
construction.com

Green Pads, LLC
www.greenpads.com

Kent Taylor Construction
1517 Crest Avenue
Richmond, CA 94805
510.703.0423

Kevin Donahue Structural Engineer
1101 – 8th Street
Berkeley, CA 94710
510.528.5394

Heidi Hansen Architecture
3463 Wellesly Avenue
San Diego, CA 92122
858.452.2157

Lindy Small Architecture
95 Linden Street, No. 10
Oakland, CA 94607
510.251.1066
www.lindysmallarchitecture.com

Michael Heacock + Associates
1591 B Stillwell Road
San Francisco, CA 94129
415.845.5326
www.michaelheacock.com

Rempel Architects
1819 – 5th Street
Berkeley, CA 94710
510.845.9777

Richard Beller
228 Los Cerros Drive
San Luis Obispo, CA
805.541.5741

Russell Johnson
3289 Veteran Avenue
Los Angeles, CA 90034
310.470.1948
www.tritechdesign.com
Russell.Johnson@verizon.net

San Luis Sustainability Group
SLOSG@slonet.org
www.slosustainability.com

Thompson/Naylor Architects
900 Philinda Avenue
Santa Barbara, CA 93103
805.966.9807
www.thompsonnaylor.com

Toby Long
Clever Homes, LLC
665 Third Street
San Francisco, CA 94107
415.344.0806
www.cleverhomes.net

State Organizations

Alabama

Alabama Solar Energy Center
University of Alabama at Huntsville
Johnson Research Center
Huntsville, AL 35899
256.890.6343
800.874.3327 (in Alabama)
Fax: 256.890.6848

Energy, Weatherization
and Technology Division
Department of Economic and
Community Affairs
401 Adams Avenue
P.O. Box 5690
Montgomery, AL 36103
334.242.5100
Fax: 334.242.5099
www.adeca.state.al.us/EWT/
default.aspx

Alaska

Alaska Energy Authority
Alaska Industrial Development
and Export Authority
813 West Northern Lights
Boulevard
Anchorage, AK 99503
907.269.3000
Fax: 907.269.3044
www.aidea.org/aea/index.html

American Samoa

Territorial Energy Office
American Samoa Government
Samoa Energy House, Tauna
Pago Pago, AS 96799
684.699.1101
Fax: 684.699.2835

www.americansamoa.gov/
departments/offices/energy.htm

Arizona

Arizona Department of Commerce
1700 West Washington, Suite 220
Phoenix, AZ 85007
602.771.1201
Fax: 602.771.1203
www.azcommerce.com/Energy/

Arkansas

Arkansas Energy Office
Arkansas Department of
Economic Development
One Capitol Mall, Suite 4B-215
Little Rock, AR 72201
501.682.1370
Fax: 501.682.2703
Energy@1800arkansas.com
www.1800arkansas.com/Energy/

California

California Energy Commission
1516 Ninth Street, MS #39
Sacramento, CA 95814
916.654.4058
Fax: 916.654.4423
www.energy.ca.gov

The Real Goods Solar Living Institute
13771 South Highway 101
P.O. Box 836
Hopland, CA 95449
707.744.2017
www.solarliving.org/

Colorado

Governor's Energy Office
225 East 16th Avenue, Suite 650
Denver, CO 80203
303.866.2100
Fax: 303.866.2930
geo@state.co.us
www.state.co.us/oemc

Connecticut

Connecticut Clean Energy Fund
200 Corporate Place, 3rd Floor
Rocky Hill, CT 06067
860.563.0015
Fax: 860.563.6978
www.ctinnovations.com

Energy & Policy Unit, PDPD
Connecticut Office of Policy
and Management
450 Capitol Avenue, MS #52 ENR
P.O. Box 341441
Hartford, CT 06134
860.418.6200
Fax: 860.418.6487
www.opm.state.ct.us/pdpd2/
energy/enserv.htm

Delaware

Delaware Energy Office
1203 College Park Drive, Suite 101
Dover, DE 19904
302.735.3480
Fax: 302.739.1840
www.delaware-energy.com

District of Columbia

D.C. Energy Office
2000 14th Street NW,
Suite 300 East
Washington, D.C. 20009
202.673.6700
Fax: 202.673.6725
www.dceo.dc.gov/dceo/site/
default.asp

Florida

Florida Energy Office
Florida Department of
Environmental Protection
3900 Commonwealth Boulevard,
MS #19
Tallahassee, FL 32399
850.245.8002
Fax: 850.245.2947
www.dep.state.fl.us/energy/
default.htm

Florida Solar Energy Center
1679 Clearlake Road
Cocoa, FL 32922
407.638.1000
Fax: 407.638.1010
webmaster@fsec.ucf.edu
www.fsec.ucf.edu

Georgia

Division of Energy Resources
Georgia Environmental Facilities
Authority
233 Peachtree Street NE
Harris Tower, Suite 900
Atlanta, GA 30303
404.584.1000
Fax: 404.584.1069
www.gefa.org/Index.aspx?page=32

Guam

Guam Energy Office
548 North Marine Corps Drive
Tamuning, Guam 96913
671.646.4361
Fax: 671.649.1215
www.guamenergy.com/main/
index.php?pg=contact
www.guamenergy.com/

Hawaii

Strategic Industries Division
Department of Business, Economic
Development and Tourism
235 South Beretania Street,
Room 502
P.O. Box 2359
Honolulu, HI 96804
808.587.3812
Fax: 808.586.2536
library@dbedt.hawaii.gov
www.hawaii.gov/dbedt/info/energy/

Idaho

Energy Division
Idaho Department of
Water Resources
322 East Front Street

P.O. Box 83720
Boise, ID 83720
208.287.4800
Fax: 208.287.6700
energyspecialist@idwr.idaho.gov
www.idwr.idaho.gov/energy/

Illinois

Energy & Recycling Bureau
Illinois Department of Commerce
and Economic Opportunity
620 East Adams
Springfield, IL 62701
217.785.3416
Fax: 217.785.2618
www.commerce.state.il.us/dceo/
Bureaus/Energy_Recycling/

Indiana

Office of Energy and Defense
Development
101 West Ohio Street, Suite 1250
Indianapolis, IN 46204
317.232.8939
Fax: 317.232.8995
www.energy.in.gov

Iowa

Energy & Waste Management
Bureau
Iowa Department of
Natural Resources
Wallace State Office Building
502 East 9th Street
Des Moines, IA 50319
515.281.8912
Fax: 515.281.8895
www.iowadnr.com/energy/
index.html

Kansas

Kansas Energy Office
Kansas Corporation Commission
1500 Southwest Arrowhead Road
Topeka, KS 66604
785.271.3170
Fax: 785.271.3268

public.affairs@kcc.state.ks.us
www.kcc.ks.gov/energy/

Kentucky

Governor's Office of Energy Policy
Division of Renewable Energy
Energy Efficiency
500 Mero Street, 12th Floor
Capital Plaza Tower
Frankfort, KY 40601
502.564.7192
Fax: 504.564.7484
marie.anthony@ky.gov
www.energy.ky.gov/default.htm

Louisiana

Technology Assessment Division
Department of Natural Resources
P.O. Box 94396
617 North Third Street
Baton Rouge, LA 70804
225.342.1399
Fax: 225.342.1397
techasmt@la.gov
ww.dnr.louisiana.gov/techasmt

Maine

State Energy Program
Maine Public Utilities Commission
State House Station No. 18
Augusta, ME 04333
207.287.3318
Fax: 207.287.1039
joy.adamson@maine.gov
www.state.maine.gov/msep

Maryland

Maryland Energy Administration
1623 Forest Drive, Suite 300
Annapolis, MD 21403
410.260.7655
Fax: 410.974.2250
meainfo@energy.state.md.us
www.energy.state.md.us

Massachusetts

Division of Energy Resources
  Executive Office of Energy &
    Environmental Affairs
  100 Cambridge Street, Suite 1020
  Boston, MA 02114
  617.727.4732
  Fax: 617.727.0030
  DOER.Energy@state.ma.us
  www.mass.gov/doer/

Michigan

Energy Office
  Michigan Department of Labor
    & Economic Growth
  P.O. Box 30221
  611 West Ottawa, 4th Floor
  Lansing, MI 48909
  517.241.6228
  Fax: 517.241.6229
  erdinfo@michigan.gov
  www.michigan.gov/energyoffice

Minnesota

State Energy Office
  Minnesota Department of
    Commerce
  85 – 7th Place East, Suite 600
  St. Paul, MN 55101
  651.296.4026
  Fax: 651.297.7891
  energy.info@state.mn.us
  www.commerce.state.mn.us

Mississippi

Energy Division
  Mississippi Development Authority
  P.O. Box 849
  510 George Street, Suite 300
  Jackson, MS 39205
  601.359.6600
  Fax: 601.359.6642
  energydiv@mississippi.org
  www.mississippi.org/content.aspx
    ?url=/page/3331&

Missouri

Energy Center
  Department of Natural Resources
  P.O. Box 176
  1101 Riverside Drive
  Jefferson City, MO 65102
  573.751.2254
  Fax: 573.751.6860
  energy@dnr.mo.gov
  www.dnr.mo.gov/energy/index.html

Montana

Department of Environmental Quality
  P.O. Box 200901
  1100 North Last Chance Gulch,
  Room 401-H
  Helena, MT 59620
  406.841.5240
  Fax: 406.841.5222
  www.deq.state.mt.us/energy/

Nebraska

Nebraska State Energy Office
  111 "O" Street, Suite 223
  Lincoln, NE 68508
  402.471.2867
  Fax: 402.471.3064
  energy@neo.ne.gov
  www.neo.ne.gov

Nevada

Nevada State Office of Energy
  727 Fairview Drive, Suite F
  Carson City, NV 89701
  775.687.9700
  Fax: 775.687.9714
  www.energy.state.nv.us

New Hampshire

Office of Energy and Planning
  State of New Hampshire
  57 Regional Drive, Suite 3
  Concord, NH 03301
  603.271.2155
  Fax: 603.271.2615
  www.nh.gov/oep/

New Jersey

Office of Clean Energy
  New Jersey Board of Public Utilities
  44 South Clinton Avenue
  P.O. Box 350
  Trenton, NJ 08625
  609.777.3300
  Fax: 609.777.3330
  energy@bpu.state.nj.us
  www.bpu.state.nj.us

New Mexico

Energy Conservation
  and Management Division
  New Mexico Energy, Minerals and
    Natural Resources Department
  1220 South St. Francis Drive
  P.O. Box 6429
  Santa Fe, NM 87505
  505.476.3311
  Fax: 505.476.3322
  emnrd.ecmd@state.nm.us
  www.emnrd.state.nm.us/ecmd/

New York

New York State Energy Research
  and Development Authority
  17 Columbia Circle
  Albany, NY 12203
  518.862.1090
  Fax: 518.862.1091
  www.nyserda.org

North Carolina

State Energy Office
  North Carolina Department of
    Administration
  1340 Mail Service Center
  Raleigh, NC 27699
  919.733.2230
  Fax: 919.733.2953
  energyinfo@ncmail.net
  www.energync.net

North Dakota

Office of Renewable
  Energy & Energy Efficiency
  North Dakota Department
    of Commerce
  P.O. Box 2057
  1600 East Century Avenue, Suite 2
  Bismarck, ND 58502
  703.328.5300
  Fax: 701.328.2308
  dcs@nd.gov
  www.ndcommerce.com/

Northern Mariana Islands

Energy Division
  Commonwealth of the
    Northern Mariana Islands
  P.O. Box 500340
  Saipan, NMI 96950
  670.664.4480
  Fax: 670.664.4483
  energy@pticom.com
  www.net.saipan.com/cftem
    plates/executive/index.cfm?
    pageID=20

Ohio

Office of Energy Efficiency
  Ohio Department of Development
  P.O. Box 1001
  77 South High Street, 26th Floor
  Columbus, OH 43216
  614.466.6797
  Fax: 614.466.1864
  pboone@odod.state.oh.us
  www.odod.state.oh.us/cdd/oee/

Oklahoma

Office of Community Development
  Oklahoma Department
    of Commerce
  P.O. Box 26980
  900 North Stiles
  Oklahoma City, OK 73126
  405.815.6552
  Fax: 405.605.2870
  www.okcommerce.gov

Oregon

Oregon Department of Energy
625 Marion Street, Northeast
Salem, OR 97301
503.378.4040
Fax: 503.373.7806
energy.in.internet@state.or.us
www.oregon.gov/ENERGY/

Pennsylvania

Pennsylvania Bureau of Energy,
Innovations, & Technology
Deployment
Department of Environmental
Protection

P.O. Box 8772
Harrisburg, PA 17105
717.783.0540
Fax: 717.783.2703
eppaenergy@state.pa.us
www.depweb.state.pa.us/energy

Puerto Rico

Energy Affairs Administration
P.O. Box 366147
Puerta de Tierra Station
San Juan, PR 00936
787.999.2200, ext. 2888
Fax: 787.753.2220
mvillanueva@drna.gobierno.pr
www.aae.gobierno.pr/

Rhode Island

Rhode Island Office of Energy
Resources
1 Capitol Hill, 2nd Floor
Providence, RI 02908
401.574.9100
Fax: 401.574.9125
www.riseo.ri.gov

South Carolina

South Carolina Energy Office
1201 Main Street, Suite 430
Columbia, SC 29201
803.737.8030

Fax: 803.737.9846
www.energy.sc.gov/

South Dakota

Energy Management Office
Bureau of Administration
523 East Capitol Avenue
Pierre, SD 57501
605.773.3899
Fax: 605.773.5980
BOAGeneralInformation
@state.sd.us
www.state.sd.us/boa/ose/OSE_
Statewide_Energy.htm

Tennessee

Energy Policy Section
Department of Economic &
Community Development
312 – 8th Avenue North,
10th Floor
Nashville, TN 37243
615.741.2373
Fax: 615.741.0607
www.state.tn.us/ecd/energy.htm

Texas

State Energy Conservation Office
Texas Comptroller of Public
Accounts
111 East 17th Street, #1114
Austin, TX 78701
512.463.1931
Fax: 512.475.2569
www.seco.cpa.state.tx.us/

Utah

Utah State Energy Program
Utah Geological Survey
P.O. Box 14610
1594 West North Temple,
Suite 3110
Salt Lake City, UT 84114
801.537.3300
Fax: 801.538.4795
dbeaudoin@utah.gov
www.energy.utah.gov

Vermont

Efficiency Vermont
255 South Champlain Street, Suite
7
Burlington, VT 05401
888.921.5990
www.efficiencyvermont.com

Energy Efficiency Division
Vermont Department of Public
Service
112 State Street, Drawer 20
Montpelier, VT 05620
802.828.2811
Fax: 802.828.2342
vtdps@psd.state.vt.us
www.publicservice.vermont.gov/
divisions/energy-efficiency.html

Vermont Green Building Network
P.O. Box 5384
Burlington, VT 05402
802.338.7664
info@VGBN.org
www.vgbn.org

Vermont Public Interest Research
Group
141 Main Street, Suite 6
Montpelier, VT 05602
802.223.5221
vpirg@vpirg.org
www.vpirg.org

Virginia

Division of Energy
Virginia Department of Mines,
Minerals & Energy
202 North Ninth Street, 8th Floor
Richmond, VA 23219
804.692.3200
Fax: 804.692.3237
www.dmme.virginia.gov/divi-
sionenergy.shtml

Virgin Islands

Virgin Islands Energy Office
Department of Planning and
Natural Resources

#45 Mars Hill
Frederiksted, St. Croix,
USVI 00840
340.773.1082
Fax: 340.772.0063
dbuchanan@vienergy.org
www.vienergy.org/

Washington

Washington Energy Policy Office
Washington State Office of Trade
and Economic Development
P.O. Box 43173
906 Columbia Street SW
Olympia, WA 98504
360.725.3118
Fax: 360.586.0049
www.cted.wa.gov/portal/alias__ct
ed/lang__en/tabID__526/
DesktopDefault.aspx

West Virginia

Energy Efficiency Office
West Virginia Development
Office State Capitol Complex
Building 6, Room 645
1900 Kanawha Boulevard East
Charleston, WV 25305
304.558.2234
Fax: 304.558.0362
www.wvdo.org/community/eep.html

Wisconsin

Wisconsin Office of Energy
Independence
17 West Main Street, #429
Madison, WI 53702
608.261.6609
Fax: 608.261.8427
www.power.wisconsin.gov/

Wyoming

Business & Industry Division–
State Energy Program
Wyoming Business Council
214 West 15th Street
Cheyenne, WY 82002

307.777.2800
Fax: 307.777.2837
tfuller@wybusiness.org
www.wyomingbusiness.org/
business/energy.aspx

National Associations & Renewable Energy Industry Groups

American Society of Heating, Refrigeration, and Air Conditioning Engineers (ASHRAE)
1791 Tullie Circle NE
Atlanta, GA 30329
404.636.8400
Fax: 404.321.5478
ashrae@ashrae.org
www.ashrae.org

American Solar Energy Society
2400 Central Avenue, Unit G-1
Boulder, CO 80301
303.443.3130
Fax: 303.443.3212
ases@ases.org
www.ases.org

Office of Energy Efficiency and Renewable Energy
P.O. Box 3048
Merrifield, VA 22116
800.523.2929
800.363.3732
Fax: 703.893.0400
doe.erec@nciinc.com
www.eere.energy.gov/

Hydronic Radiant Heating Association
123 C Street
Davis, CA 95616
530.753.1100
Fax: 530.753.4125

National Association of State Energy Officials (NASEO)
1414 Prince Street, Suite 200
Alexandria, VA 22314

703.299.8800
Fax: 703.299.6208
mnew@naseo.org
www.naseo.org/

National Association of Regulatory and Utility Commissioners (NARUC)
1101 Vermont, Northwest, Suite 200
Washington, D.C. 20005
202.898.2200
Fax: 202.898.2213
www.naruc.org

National Renewable Energy Laboratory
1617 Cole Boulevard
Golden, CO 80401
303.275.3000
Fax: 303.275.4053
webmaster@nrel.gov
www.nrel.gov

Solar Energy Industries Association
122 C Street NW, 4th Floor
Washington, D.C. 20001
202.383.2600
Fax: 202.383.2670
info@seia.org
www.seia.org

Solar Energy Industries Association (SEIA)
1616 H Street NW, Suite 800
Washington, D.C. 20006
202.628.7745
Fax: 202.628.7779
www.seia.org

Sustainable Buildings Industry Council
1112 – 16th Street NW, Suite 240
Washington, D.C. 20036
Voicemail: 202.628.7400
Fax: 202.393.5043
sbic@sbicouncil.org
www.sbicouncil.org

Other Organizations

Center for Renewable Energy & Sustainable Technology
1612 K Street NW, Suite 202
Washington, D.C. 20006
202.293.2898
Fax: 202.293.5857
info@crest.org
www.crest.org

National Energy Education Development Project
8408 Kao Circle
Manassas, VA 20110
703.257.1117
Fax: 703.257.0037
info@need.org
www.need.org

National Energy Foundation
3676 California Avenue, Suite A117
Salt Lake City, UT 84104
801.908.5800
Fax: 801.908.5400
info@nef1.org
www.nef1.org

National Energy Information Center
U.S. Department of Energy
Energy Information
   Administration, EI30
1000 Independence Avenue SW
Washington, D.C. 20585
202.586.8800
infoctr@eia.doe.gov
www.eia.doe.gov

N.C. Solar Energy Association
P.O. Box 6465
Raleigh, NC 27628
919.832.7601
ncsea@mindspring.com
www.ncsolar.org

Northeast Sustainable Energy Association
50 Miles Street
Greenfield, MA 01301
413.774.6051

nesea@nesea.org
www.nesea.org

Solar Cookers International
1919 – 21st Street, Suite 101
Sacramento, CA 95814
916.455.4499
Fax: 916.455.4498
info@solarcookers.org
www.solarcooking.org

Solar Energy Industries Association
805 – 15th Street NW, Suite 510
Washington, D.C. 20005
202.628.0556
202.628.7779
info@seia.org
www.seia.org

Solar Now Project
100 Sohier Road
Beverly, MA 01915
978.927.9786
Fax: 978.927.9191
solarnow@mediaone.net
www.solarnow.org

Southface Energy Institute
241 Pine Street
Atlanta, GA 30308
404.872.3549
Fax: 404.872.5009
questions@southface.org
www.southface.org

Union of Concerned Scientists
2 Brattle Square
Cambridge, MA 02238
617.547.5552
Fax: 617.864.9405
ucs@ucsusa.org
www.ucsusa.org

University of Central Florida
Regional Service Project III
College of Education, Room 146
Orlando, FL 32816
407.823.2950
RSP3@pegasus.cc.ucf.edu

Other Helpful Web Sites

Environmental Building News
www.buildinggreen.com

Million Solar Roofs Initiative
www.millionsolarroofs.com

National Center for Photovoltaics
www.nrel.gov/ncpv

Renewable Energy Access
www.renewableenergyaccess.com/rea/home

Renewable Resource Data Center
www.rredc.nrel.gov/

Solar Energy Technologies Program
www.eere.energy.gov/solar

Conservation & Efficiency Resources

Building America Program
U.S. Department of Energy
www.eere.energy.gov/buildings/building_america

Database of State Incentives for Renewables and Efficiency
www.dsireusa.org

The Energy Conservatory
2801 – 21st Avenue, South, Suite 160
Minneapolis, MN 55407
612.827.1117
Fax: 612.827.1051
info@energyconservatory.com
www.energyconservatory.com

Energy Star
1200 Pennsylvania Avenue NW
Washington, D.C. 20460
888.STAR.YES
www.energystar.gov/homes

Information on proper CFL disposal
www.lamprecycle.org
www.earth911.org
www.nema.org/lamprecycle/epafactsheet-cfl.pdf

Residential Energy Services Network (RESNET)
P.O. Box 4561
Oceanside, CA 92052
760.806.3448
Fax: 760.806.9449
info@natresnet.org
www.natresnet.org

Tax Incentives Assistance Project (TIAP)
www.energytaxincentives.org

Passive Heating & Cooling Resources

American Solar Energy Society
2400 Central Avenue, Suite A
Boulder, CO 80301
303.443.3130
Fax: 303.443.3212
ases@ases.org
www.ases.org

Office of Energy Efficiency and Renewable Energy
P.O. Box 3048
Merrifield, VA 22116
800.523.2929
800.363.3732
Fax: 703.893.0400
doe.erec@nciinc.com
www.eere.energy.gov/

Florida Solar Energy Center
University of Central Florida
1679 Clearlake Road
Cocoa, FL 32922
407.638.1000
Fax: 407.638.1010
infor@fsec.ucf.edu
www.fsec.ucf.edu

Home Energy Saver
www.hes.lbl.gov/

National Association of Home Builders-Research Foundation
400 Prince George Boulevard
Upper Marlboro, MD 20774
800.638.8556
Fax: 301.249.3035
info@nahb.com
www.nahbrc.org

National Center for Appropriate Technology
P.O. Box 3838
3040 Continental Drive
Butte, MT 59702
800.275.6228
406.494.4572
Fax: 406.494.2905
info@ncat.org
www.ncat.org

National Climatic Data Center
www.ncdc.noaa.gov/oa/ncdc.html

National Renewable Energy Laboratory (NREL)
1617 Cole Boulevard
Golden, CO 80401
303.275.3000
Fax: 303.275.4053
www.nrel.gov

North Carolina Solar Center
P.O. Box 7401
North Carolina State University
Raleigh, NC 27695
919.515.5666
800.33.NCSUN (toll-free in NC)
Fax: 919.515.5778
ncsun@ncsu.edu
www.ncsc.ncsu.edu/

North Carolina Solar Energy Association
2501 Blue Ridge Road, Suite 150
Raleigh, NC 27607
919.832.7601
Fax: 919.863.4101
www.ncsolar.org

Passive Solar Industries Council (PSIC)
1331 H Street NW, Suite 1000
Washington, D.C. 20005
202.628.7400
Fax: 202.393.5043
PSICouncil@aol.com
www.psic.org/

Solar Thermal Design Assistance Center
Sandia National Laboratories
Mail Stop 0703
Albuquerque, NM 87185
505.844.3077
Fax: 505.844.7786
dfmenic@sandia.gov
www.sandia.gov/Renewable_Energy/solarthermal/dufdac.html

Southface Energy Institute
241 Pine Street
Atlanta, GA 30308
404.872.3549
Fax: 404.872.5009
info@southface.org
www.southface.org

Sustainable Building Industries Council
1331 H Street NW, Suite 1000
Washington, D.C. 20005
202.628.7400
Fax: 202.393.5043
sbicouncil@sbicouncil.org
www.sbicouncil.org

Solar Domestic Hot Water Resources

Database of State Incentives for Renewables and Efficiency (DSIRE)
www.dsireusa.org

Hot Water Savings Tips
www.rredc.nrel.gov/solar/codes_algs/ PVWATTS

Solar Rating and Certification Corporation (SRCC)
www.solar-rating.org

U.S. DOE, Office of Energy
Efficiency and Renewable Energy
www.eere.energy.gov/consumer/
your_home/water_heating/
index.cfm/mytopic=12760

Solar Space Heating Resources

American Society of Heating,
Refrigeration, and Air Conditioning
Engineers (ASHRAE)
1791 Tullie Circle NE
Atlanta, GA 30329
404.636.8400
Fax: 404.321.5478
ashrae@ashrae.org
www.ashrae.org

American Solar Energy Society
2400 Central Avenue, Suite A
Boulder, CO 80301
303.443.3130
Fax: 303.443.3212
ases@ases.org
www.ases.org/solar

Hydronic Radiant Heating Association
123 C Street
Davis, CA 95616
530.753.1100
Fax: 530.753.4125

National Renewable Energy
Laboratory
1617 Cole Boulevard
Golden, CO 80401
303.275.3000
Fax: 303.275.4053
webmaster@nrel.gov
www.nrel.gov

Solar Energy Industries Association
805 – 15th Street NW, Suite 510
Washington, D.C. 20005
202.682.0556
Fax: 202.682.7779
info@seia.org
www.seia.org

Solar Thermal Design Assistance
Center
Sandia National Laboratories
Mail Stop 0703
Albuquerque, NM 87185
505.844.3077
Fax: 505.844.7786
dfmenic@sandia.gov
www.sandia.gov/Renewable_
Energy/solarthermal/dufdac.html

Biomass

HearthNet: Advice from wood-fired
central heating experts.
www.hearth.com

Pellet Fuels Institute
1901 North Moore Street,
Suite 600
Arlington, VA 22209
703.522.6778
www.pelletheat.org

Woodheat.org: Extensive information about heating with wood.
www.woodheat.org

Biodiesel

National Biodiesel Board
3337A Emerald Lane
P.O. Box 104898
Jefferson City, MO 65110
800.841.5849
573.635.3893
Fax: 573.635.7913
info@biodiesel.org
www.biodiesel.org

Solar Electricity Resources

American Solar Energy Society
2400 Central Avenue, Suite A
Boulder, CO 80301
303.443.3130
Fax: 303.443.3212
ases@ases.org
www.ases.org

Energy Efficiency and Renewable
Energy Clearinghouse (EREC)
P.O. Box 3048
Merrifield, VA 2216
800.523.2929
Fax: 703.893-0400
doe.erec@nciinc.com
www.eren.energy.gov

Florida Solar Energy Center
University of Central Florida
1679 Clearlake Road
Cocoa, FL 32922
407.638.1000
Fax: 407.638.1010
infor@fsec.ucf.edu
www.fsec.ucf.edu

National Association of Home
Builders (NAHB) Research
Foundation
400 Prince George Boulevard
Upper Marlboro, MD 20774
800.638.8556
Fax: 301.249.3035
info@nahb.com
www.nahbrc.org

National Center for Appropriate
Technology
P.O. Box 3838
3040 Continental Drive
Butte, MT 59702
800.275.6228
406.494.4572
Fax: 406.494.2905
info@ncat.org
www.ncat.org

National Renewable Energy
Laboratory (NREL)
1617 Cole Boulevard
Golden, CO 80401
303.275.3000
Fax: 303.275.4053
www.nrel.gov

North Carolina Solar Energy
Association
2501 Blue Ridge Road, Suite 150
Raleigh, NC 27607

919.832.7601
Fax: 919.863.4101
ncsea@mindspring.com
www.ncsolar.org

Northeast Sustainable Energy
Association
50 Miles Street
Greenfield, MA 01301
413.774.6051
nesea@nesea.org
www.nesea.org

Wind Power Resources

The American Wind Energy
Association
1101 – 14th Street NW,
12th Floor
Washington, D.C. 20005
202.383.2500
Fax: 202.383.2505
windmail@awea.org
www.awea.org.

National Oceanic and Atmospheric
Association
www.ncdc.noaa.gov/oa/climate/
online/ccd/wndspd.tx

National Wind Coordinating
Committee
www.nationalwind.org

Northwest Sustainable Energy for
Economic Development (SEED)
www.nwseed.org

Searchable Directory of Wind and
Renewable Energy Companies and
Products Worldwide
www.energy.sourceguides.com
/index.shtml

Solar Energy International
970.963.8855
www.solarenergy.org

State and local wind power sites
www.eere.energy.gov/RE/wind-state.html
www.eere.energy.gov/windand
hydro/windpoweringamerica/

Wind Power Maps
www.windpowermaps.org

Windustry
info@windustry.org
www.windustry.com

Financing, Incentive & Rebate Resources

Clean Energy
U.S. Environmental
Protection Agency
1200 Pennsylvania Avenue NW,
MC #6202J
Washington, D.C. 20460
202.343.9442
critchfield.james@epa.gov
www.epa.gov/cleanenergy/

Database of state incentives for
renewable energy
www.dsireusa.org/

Interstate Renewable Energy
Council (IREC)
P.O. Box 1156
Latham, NY 12110
518.458.6059
info@irecusa.org
www.irecusa.org

Renewable Energy System Design & Installation Resources

Databases of Installers
www.gosolar.com
www.homepower.com/resources/
directory.cfm
www.renewableenergyaccess.
com/rea/market/business/home
www.seia.org/statechapters.php

North American Board of Certified
Energy Practitioners (NABCEP)
Saratoga Technology
& Energy Park
10 Hermes Road, Suite 400
Malta, NY 12020
518.899.8186
info@nabcep.org
www.nabcep.org

The Source for Renewable Energy
www.energy.sourceguides.com/
index.shtml

Bibliography & Recommended Reading

Bickford, Carl. "Sizing Solar Hot Water Systems." *Home Power* 118, April/May 2007.

Blaylock, Forrest E. "Solar Heating in the North." *Home Power* 115, October/November 2006.

Brower, Michael, PhD, and Warren Leon PhD. *The Consumer's Guide to Effective Environmental Choices: Practical Advice from the Union of Concerned Scientists.* New York: Three Rivers Press, 1999.

Casale, Dan. "Prepaid Power: Putting Renewables to Work for You." *Home Power* 116, December 2006/January 2007.

Chiras, Dan. *The Homeowner's Guide to Renewable Energy.* Gabriola Island, BC: New Society Publishers, 2006.

————. *The Natural House: A Complete Guide to Healthy, Energy-Efficient, Environmental Homes.* White River Junction, VT: Chelsea Green Publishing, 2000.

Chisholm, Grey. "Finding True South the Easy Way." *Home Power* 120, August/September 2007.

Coleman, Debra Rucker. "Designing Your Place in the Sun." *Home Power* 116, December 2006/January 2007.

Cox, Ben, and Sandra Zaslow. *Passive Solar Options for North Carolina Homes.* North Carolina Solar Center, North Carolina State University, SC102, December 1999.

Cunningham, Paul, and Ian Woofenden. "MicroHydro-Electric Systems Simplified." *Home Power* 117, February/March 2007.

Deri, Sacha. "A Renewable Energy Primer: Choosing the Source That's Right for You." *Green Living*, Spring 2007.

Do It Yourself Solar Applications: For Water and Space Heating. North Carolina Solar Center, North Carolina State University, SC123, June 2000.

Eberle, Mary. "Wiser Water Use." *Home Power* 120, August/September 2007.

The Editors of *E Magazine, Green Living*, New York: Plume, 2005.

Energy Education Resources for Teachers and Students. North Carolina Solar Center, North Carolina State University, SC118, Revised September 2001.

Garst, Sam. "Advancing a Green Dream," *Solar Today*, March/April 2007.

Get Your Power from the Sun: A Consumer's Guide. U.S. Department of Energy, December 2003.

Gipe, Paul. *Wind Energy Basics: A Guide to Small and Micro Wind Systems.* White River Junction, VT: Chelsea Green Publishing Company, 1999.

Hammett, Dr. Wilma. *Decorating Your Passive Solar Home: Balancing Energy and Aesthetics.* North Carolina Solar Center, North Carolina State University, SC100, June 2000.

Higginson, Charles. "Easy DIY Solar Lighting." *Mother Earth News*, April/May 2007.

Horn, Doug. "Energy Smarts: Efficiency Gains + Solar Electricity." *Home Power* 119, June/July 2007.

Howard, Brian C. "Keep Your Cool With Less AC." *The Green Guide*, July/August 2007.

Kachadorian, James. *The Passive Solar House: Using Solar Design to Heat & Cool Your Home.* White River Junction, VT: Chelsea Green Publishing Company, 1997.

Kerr, Andy. "Making Sense & Dollars of Solar Hot Air Collectors." *Home Power* 118, April/May 2007.

Lane, Tom, and Ken Olson. "Solar Hot Water for Cold Climates, Part 2: Drainback Systems." *Home Power* 86, December 2001/January 2002.

Livingston, Phil. "First Steps in Renewable Energy for Your Home." *Home Power* 118, April/May 2007.

"Mapping Energy Needs with Renewable Energy Resources." *Home Power* 116, December 2006/January 2007.

Marken, Chuck, and Ken Olsen. "Installation Basics for Solar Domestic Water Heating Systems." *Home Power* 94, April/May 2003.

———. "SDHW Basics, Part 2: Closed-Loop Antifreeze." *Home Power* 95, June/July 2003.

Marsden, Guy. "Solar Heat: Expanding & Upgrading an Owner Installed System." *Home Power* 119, June/July 2007.

Maurer, Christine C.; Alex Hobbs, PhD., PE; and Steve Kalland. *Guide to Interconnecting Small PV Systems for Participation in NC Green Power.* North Carolina Solar Center, North Carolina State University, Revision 1: November 2004.

McKibben, Bill. "Green from the Ground Up." *Sierra*, July/August 2007.

Morris, Stephen. *The New Village Green.* Gabriola Island, BC: New Society Publishers, 2007.

Newman, Nell, with Joseph D'Agnese. *The Newman's Own Organics Guide to the Good Life: Simple Measures that Benefit You and the Place You Live.* New York: Villard Books, 2003.

Olson, Ken. "Solar Hot Water for Cold Climates: Closed-Loop Antifreeze System Components." *Home Power* 85, October/November 2001.

———. "Solar Hot Water: A Primer." *Home Power* 84, August/September 2001.

Pahl, Greg. *Natural Home Heating: The Complete Guide to Renewable Energy Options.* White River Junction, VT: Chelsea Green Publishing, 2003.

———. "New and Improved Wind Power." *Mother Earth News*, June/July 2007.

———. *The Citizen-Powered Energy Handbook: Community Solutions to a Global Crisis.* White River Junction, VT: Chelsea Green Publishing, 2007.

Passive and Active Solar Domestic Hot Water Systems. North Carolina Solar Center, North Carolina State University, SC122, Revised June 2002.

Passive Cooling for Your North Carolina Home. North Carolina Solar Center, North Carolina State University, SC113, April 2000.

Passive Solar Home Design Checklist. North Carolina Solar Center, North Carolina State University, SC122, Revised June 2002.

Patterson, John. "Solar Hot Water Simplified." *Home Power* 107, June/July 2005.

Pearson, David. *The New Natural House Book: Creating a Healthy, Harmonious, and Ecologically Sound Home.* New York: Fireside/Simon & Schuster, 1998.

Pinkham, Linda. "Greener Houses: A Guide Through the Alphabet Soup." *Green Living*, Summer 2007.

Reid, Lib, and Donna Stankus, *Energy-Saving Landscaping for Your Passive Solar Home.* North Carolina Solar Center, North Carolina State University, SC109, June 2001.

Reysa, Gary. "The Half Plan, Reducing Your Carbon Footprint Part Two: Reducing Your Waste Line." *Home Power* 119, June/July 2007.

———. "Passive Solar Retrofit in a Weekend." *Home Power* 117, February/March 2007.

———. "Solar Heating Plan for Any Home." *Mother Earth News*, December 2007/January 2008.

———. "The Half Plan, Reducing Your Carbon Footprint Part One: Thermal Gains." *Home Power* 118, April/May 2007.

———. "The Half Plan, Reducing Your Carbon Footprint Part Three: Defeating Drafts & Improving Insulation." *Home Power* 120, August/September 2007.

Ridlington, Elizabeth, James Moore, and Melissa Bailey. *Building Solutions: Energy Efficient Homes Save Money and Reduce Global Warming.* Vermont Public Interest Research Group, Fall 2006.

Schaeffer, John. *The Real Goods Solar Living Sourcebook.* Gabriola Island, BC: New Society Publishers, 2005.

Scheckel, Paul. "Efficiency Details for a Clean Energy Change." *Home Power* 121, October/November 2007.

———. *The Home Energy Diet.* Gabriola Island, BC: New Society Publishers, 2005.

Schwartz, Joe. "Finding the Phantoms: Eliminate Standby Energy Loss." *Home Power* 117, February/March 2007.

Sharp, Jon, Ray Furse, and Robert Chew, "Solar Success in the Northeast." *Home Power* 121, October/November 2007.

Stone, Laurie. "Home Green Home." *Home Power* 115, October/November 2006.

Trask, Crissy. *It's Easy Being Green: A Handbook for Earth-Friendly Living.* Salt Lake City, UT: Gibbs Smith, Publisher, 2006.

Venolia, Carol, and Kelly Lerner. "Forget AC!: Cool Your Home Naturally." *Mother Earth News*, August/September 2007.

———. *Natural Remodeling for the Not-So-Green House: Bringing Your Home Into Harmony with Nature.* Asheville, NC: Lark Books, 2006.

Wilson, Alex. *Your Green Home: A Guide to Planning a Healthy, Environmentally Friendly New Home.* Gabriola Island, BC: New Society Publishers, 2006.

Woofenden, Ian, and Hugh Piggott. "Anatomy of a Wind Turbine." *Home Power* 116, December 2006/January 2007.

Woofenden, Ian, and Mick Sagrillo. "How to Buy a Wind Electric System," *Home Power* 122, December 2007/January 2008.

Woofenden, Ian, with Chris LaForge. "Getting Started with Renewable Energy: Professional Load Analysis & Site Survey." *Home Power* 120, August/September 2007.

Renewable Energy & Green Living Periodicals

BackHome Magazine
P.O. Box 70
Hendersonville, NC 28793
800.992.2546
info@backhomemagazine.com
www.backhomemagazine.com/

Backwoods Home Magazine
P.O. Box 712
Gold Beach, OR 97444
541.247.8900
Fax: 541.247.8600
editor@backwoodshome.com
www.backwoodshome.com/
    index.html

E Magazine
28 Knight Street
Norwalk, CT 06851
203.854.5559
Fax: 203.866.0602
info@emagazine.com
www.emagazine.com

The Green Guide
The National Geographic Society
1145 – 17th Street NW
Washington, D.C. 20036
editor@thegreenguide.com
www.thegreenguide.com

Green Living
100 Gilead Brook Road
Randolph, VT 05060
802.234.9101
Fax: 901.234.9101
editor@greenlivingjournal.com
www.greenlivingjournal.com

Home Energy Magazine
2124 Kittredge Street, #95
Berkeley, CA 94704
510.524.5405
contact@homeenergy.org
www.homeenergy.org/

Home Power
P.O. Box 520
Ashland, OR 97520
800.707.6585
Fax: 541.512.0343
mailbox@homepower.com
www.homepower.com

Mother Earth News
1503 SW 42nd Street
Topeka, KS 66609
800.234.3368
Fax: 785.274.4305

Natural Home
1503 SW 42nd Street
Topeka, KS 66609
800.340.5846
www.naturalhomemagazine.com

Sierra
85 Second Street, 2nd Floor
San Francisco, CA 94105
415.977.5500
Fax: 415.977.5799
sierra.magazine@sierraclub.org
www.sierraclub.org

Solar Today
2400 Central Avenue, Suite A
Boulder, CO 80301
303.443.3130
Fax: 303.443.3212
publisher@solartoday.org
www.solartoday.org/

Photo Credits

The authors and Gibbs Smith would like to thank the following people for their beautiful photographic contributions to this book:

AEE Solar, courtesy of: 58, 66

Georgios Alexandris, Dreamstime.com: 75

Robert Asento, 123RF Limited: 99

Avalon642, Dreamstime.com: 98

Ryszard Bednarek, 123RF Limited: 44

Anthony Berenyi, Dreamstime.com: 18

Jack Bingham: 21, 70, 79, 95, 107 (upper), 124

Cheryl Casey, Dreamstime.com, and Knud Nielsen, 123RF Limited: 32

Jonathan Davis: 41–43
  Davis Studio Architecture + Design
  13105 Venice Boulevard
  Los Angeles, CA 90066
  310.572.6055
  www.davisstudioad.com

Djole5384, Dreamstime.com: 11, 59, 127

Energy PGE, courtesy of: 103–4

Energy Systems and Design, courtesy of: 117

EPA, courtesy of: 26 (right)

Bruce Fiene: 66, 129

Richard Gunion, Dreamstime.com: 80 (left)

Cindy Haggerty, 123RF Limited: 114

Emily Hagopian: 8, 12, 13–14 (right), 16–17, 20, 24, 26, 28–30, 35–38, 45, 56–57, 60–61, 74, 76–77, 88–89, 92
  San Francisco, CA
  805.895.8756
  www.emilyhagopian.com

Ken Hurst, 123RF Limited: 25

Anne Kitzman, Dreamstime.com: 40

Aaron Kohr, Dreamstime.com: 102 (left)

Francois Lariviere, Dreamstime.com: 107 (lower)

Olivier Le Queinec, Dreamstime.com: 128 (lower)

Robert Lerich, 123RF Limited: 23, 34 (left)

Chiya Li, Dreamstime.com: 50

Aleksandr Lobanov, 123RF Limited: 19

Marlee, Dreamstime.com: 118

Maxim Miroshnichenko, Dreamstime.com: 106

Mark O'Donnell: 7, 53, 55, 80 (right)

Jim Parkin, Dreamstime.com: 94, 102 (right)

J. D. Peterson: 10, 62, 64–65, 87, 90
  2354 – 48th Avenue
  San Francisco, CA 94116
  415.681.3456
  www.jdpetersonphotography.com

Isabel Poulin, Dreamstime.com: 27 (lower)

Anthony Rich: 2–3, 48–49, 82, 84–85

Arnis Rukis, Dreamstime.com: 122

Brandon Seidel, 123RF Limited: 121

SolarRoofs.com: 81

James Steidl, Dreamstime.com: 96

Stiebel Eltron: 78, 131

Teamarbeit, Dreamstime.com: 93

Penny Williams, 123RF Limited: 108

Ulruch Willmünder, Dreamstime.com: 67, 69